THE
FORGOTTEN
WINNER

THE FORGOTTEN WINNER

The Notorious Vancouver Marathon 1954

Joe McGhee

British Empire and Commonwealth Marathon Champion 1954
Scottish Marathon Champion and
Record-holder 1954, 55 & 56

pitch

First published by Pitch Publishing, 2025
1

Pitch Publishing
9 Donnington Park,
85 Birdham Road,
Chichester, West Sussex,
PO20 7AJ
www.pitchpublishing.co.uk
info@pitchpublishing.co.uk

© 2025, Joe McGhee

Every effort has been made to trace the copyright. Any oversight will be rectified in future editions at the earliest opportunity by the publisher.

All rights reserved. No part of this book may be reproduced, sold or utilised in any form or transmitted in any form or by any means, electronic or mechanical, including photocopying, recording or by any information storage and retrieval system, without prior permission in writing from the publisher.

A CIP catalogue record is available for this book from the British Library.

ISBN 978 1 80150 956 5

Typesetting and origination by Pitch Publishing

Printed and bound on FSC® certified paper in line with our continuing commitment to ethical business practices, sustainability and the environment.

Printed and bound by CPI Group (UK) Ltd, Croydon, CR0 4YY

Contents

Foreword by Dennis Canavan MSP 9
With Thanks 11
Acknowledgements 11
Preface 13

PART A: The 1954 British Empire and Commonwealth Games Marathon and its Aftermath 1953–1960 19
1. Striving for Selection: 1953–1954 21
2. Canada: The Build-up to the Race 47
3. The British Empire and Commonwealth Marathon Race 58
4. Why Did Jim Peters Fail? 66
5. Welcome Home 73
6. A Hectic Three Months 79
7. Changing Careers 96
8. 1955 – A Year of Success 101
9. 1956 – A Year of Disappointment 124
10. Post-1956: Successes Despite Injuries 138

PART B: The Joys of Running – Then and Now . . 143
11. Five 'Inspirers' 145
12. Getting Lost 169
13. Danger to Life and Limb 183
14. The Perils of Speaking Engagements 191
15. Then and Now 199
16. Advice for Aspiring Marathon Runners 227
17. Per Ardua Ad? 232
Postscript 245
PPS: The Myths Continue 249
Bibliography 251

To Margaret

The joy of my life

The Scottish Parliament

Foreword

by Dennis Canavan MSP

Convener of the Scottish Parliament's Cross Party Sports Group

JOE McGHEE became my boyhood hero when he won the Vancouver Marathon in 1954. It was the day before my 12th birthday but Joe's famous victory is etched in my memory as if it was just yesterday.

Our family had no TV and we were very dependent on the radio and press for news of what was happening 4,000 miles away at the Empire and Commonwealth Games. The BBC and most of the English press acclaimed Jim Peters as a national hero and Joe McGhee did not get the recognition he deserved. Since then, a huge web of mythology has been spun around that famous race but two facts are undeniable: Joe ran the race to the finish and he won the gold for Scotland.

Now, half a century later, he sets the record straight by telling us how he did it.

Dennis Canavan

With Thanks

We wish to extend our sincere thanks to Dennis Canavan for kindly writing the foreword for Joe in 2004.

We also wish to thank the following for granting use of their images in the book:

Scottish Daily Express
The family of Robert G. Henderson
Shettleston Harriers
Vancouver Sun/Province

Acknowledgements

Scots Athlete – G.S Barber Photographer.
Walter J. Ross, editor of the *Scots Athlete*.

All photographs included are from Joe McGhee's own personal photograph Collection (excluding those from Alamy).

Preface

THE 1954 British Empire and Commonwealth Games Marathon has been labelled one of the ten greatest races of all time. The awful collapse of England's Jim Peters after he entered the stadium is still recalled by the media with monotonous regularity. The fact that a Scottish runner won the race is only sometimes mentioned as well.

No one would dispute Jim's sheer courage in attempting to finish. The fact is obvious in the newsreel footage taken in the stadium. Roger Bannister and I were the only athletes allowed to visit him later in hospital, and it was then that I realised how close he had come to dying. The doctor told me that he had never seen a human being so completely dehydrated. Jim and I met briefly on a *Daily Express* sports panel the following year, but we then lost contact for over 40 years until we met up again at the London Marathon's 'Notable Nineteen' Dinner in 1996 and we often discussed the race after that. He had told us in 1954 that it was only at the end of the race as he ran down the ramp into the stadium that his legs suddenly went rubbery. The doctor added quietly to me that no one could possibly have got himself into such a state in so short a time. He must have been running blindly in a state of near-collapse for some miles before. Jim, more than 40 years later, admitted to me that he had little if any memory of those last miles. Indeed, his last memory was of the final watering point – just outside the stadium, he had thought. It was, in fact, three miles back! By contrast, the same newsreel briefly shows the strength of my own finish. It is when the subsequent reports go on to tell of what happened on the roads away from the stadium, however, that we move into the realms of imaginative fiction.

The essential point to remember about the 1954 Vancouver Marathon is that it was taking place at the same time as the race between the two greatest milers and world record-breakers, Roger Bannister and John Landy. No one was going to miss seeing the much-heralded 'Miracle Mile' and, consequently, very few reporters and even team officials bothered to accompany the marathon runners. Besides, to them, the result of the marathon was a foregone conclusion: Peters, the fastest man in the world over the distance, was the absolute favourite to win. To his eternal credit, Willie Carmichael, the Scottish team manager, was one of the rare exceptions in following the race. He had inspired me to make the attempt and then timed me all the way in my record-breaking North Berwick to Edinburgh run the previous December and he certainly was not going to miss this race. Most reporters, however, simply resorted to imagination in describing the events on the Vancouver streets during the marathon.

Unfortunately, most of the myths that have grown up around the race and that have become embroidered in subsequent retellings concern my own part in it. They seem to have originated in the romantic fantasising of a local Vancouver reporter who wrote of me lying in a ditch until an old Scots lady revived me with the exhortation that the honour of Scotland was at stake! Norris McWhirter, a little later, wrote: 'Joe McGhee, an RAF officer, having fallen five times, signalled for the ambulance. While sitting in the ditch waiting for it, he heard that Peters and Cox were out of the race, so up got the bold Scot and finished the course to win.' The only true items in that statement are that I am a Scot, that I was an RAF officer and that I won the race! Over 40 years later, Norris, at a dinner in London, was to apologise to me for relying on such suspect sources. Unfortunately, the sad fact is that subsequent books and articles go on copying such second-hand, third-hand and fourth-hand flights of fantasy. Even the Amateur Athletic Association Centenary Handbook gets it wrong, as did Jim Peters in his own book. A recent newspaper article replaced the ditch-sitting by 'lying under a tree' and added gratuitously 'an inner voice' whispering, 'Come on Scotland.'

The ludicrous nature of such stories is glaringly obvious. Any athlete who has ever raced a marathon will assure you that, if you stop for more than a second or two, especially in the closing stages, you will never get started again – even more so if you have apparently decided to lie down! At no time did I 'collapse'. Indeed, I was engaged in a very active race, pulling away from the two South Africans over the last four miles and never even knew that I was first until I was just outside the stadium.

Moreover, since both Peters and Cox finished up in hospital, it was assumed that I too could not have been much better. As for my so-called state of 'exhaustion', I need only point to the press photographs of my sprinting through the tape, both feet clear of the track, then walking across the stadium afterwards with Willie Carmichael and Dr Euan Douglas, the Scottish team captain, and then the various pictures of the victory ceremony – one showing me helping the third-placed South African, Johan Barnard, whose feet were so bad that he had to be carried on a stretcher to the rostrum. The most conclusive evidence of my fitness, however, was the fact that I attended the closing ball that evening until the early hours of the morning and was up again at 6am to go to church before a trip to the USA. I suffered no after-effects and within a few weeks I was recording faster times than ever over the shorter distances and the following season I beat my Scottish record by almost ten minutes with a time of 2hrs 25mins 50secs in retaining my Scottish Marathon title. (Incidentally, this time, the fastest for any Briton in the 1955 season, still failed to win me a British vest, but the treatment of Scottish athletes by the British selectors at this period is a topic for later discussion.)

It is simply not the case that I have maintained my 'silence' as a recent press report has it. I have told my story time and time again over the years to Scottish press reporters, but even then my version often appeared distorted and the myth continues. It seems as if account is taken only of those 'reports' that have appeared in books – and, in the preparation of these, I have never at any time been approached for my account. This book, therefore, began as an attempt, among other things, to set the record straight. In avoiding any reliance on second-hand reports when I describe the 1954 Vancouver Marathon, I shall confine myself strictly to my own (first-hand) experience and try to convey to the ordinary person just what it feels like to race against an elite field in a championship marathon. It is not, then, an autobiography in the usual sense of the term. Though details of other (more important!) parts of my life may emerge, it is concerned mainly with one aspect – my love for distance running.

The first part of the book (Chapters 1 to 10) deals in depth with a period of little more than three years, 1953–54, 1955 and 1956, describing in detail my attempt to be chosen for the Empire and Commonwealth Games, the

PREFACE

Games themselves and the immediate aftermath when I was at the peak of my training and my athletic successes. It demonstrates especially the essential juggling act I had to perform, coping with the demands of work, training and social life.

The second part (Chapters 11 to 17) is concerned more generally with the humorous and at times bizarre events and personalities I encountered, compares the very different world of athletics 50 years ago with that of today and attempts to assess some of the joys of running.

PART A

The 1954 British Empire and Commonwealth Games Marathon and its Aftermath

1953–1960

Chapter 1

Striving for Selection: 1953–1954

(First Scottish Title and Record)

IT WAS not until late in 1953, the year before the Empire and Commonwealth Games, that I began to think that I might have a chance of selection for the Scottish team. On the Scottish road-racing circuit, I had won several of the shorter road races, usually about 13 or 15 miles. The most significant of these was the 'Round Dundee 15 Miles' in which I defeated for the first time Charlie Robertson of Dundee Thistle Harriers, the previous year's Scottish Marathon Champion. Two memories of that race have remained with me. As I ran round the last lap in Dens Park, I was greeted with a chorus of boos from small boys who had been expecting their local hero to win and then I was presented with the huge and truly magnificent Coronation trophy (which, incidentally, they did not put on offer the following year at the opening of the Caird Park Stadium when I again defeated Charlie, this time over the half-marathon distance, the week after my first record-breaking win in the Scottish Marathon Championship).

The problem at this time, however, was that the only full-distance marathon in Scotland was the Scottish Championship from Falkirk to Edinburgh in June 1953, and I had a bad race that day. Although I finished in third place, my best championship performance up till then, I really should have done much better. Anglo-Scot J. Duffy, Greenock man Alec MacLean and I, running together, had broken the field by the time we had reached 15 miles. Then, at 18 miles, approaching the Maybury junction at the city boundary, I had a bad spell. By 20 miles, just beyond Barnton, the first two were already almost out of sight and I was struggling on completely alone. With 2½ to 3 miles to go, someone shouted that I was 3½ minutes behind. From then on, I plodded on without hope through Leith until I reached Meadowbank Stadium and was astonished to see the leaders still running round the track. Unbelievably, I had made up over three minutes on the last 2½ miles! I at once spurted but, of course, it was far too late then and I finished third behind Duffy, the new champion, and MacLean.

I learned two valuable lessons that day that were to stand me in good stead in the years following. The first was that a race is never over until the tape is broken, as no matter how bad I might think I was, the other competitors were probably feeling much worse. The second was the vital importance of receiving information about my time in relation to other competitors during the progress of a race. That first lesson certainly stood me in good stead on that torrid day in Vancouver the following year. The second was to govern my tactics in all my following races in Scotland. My dad would start the watch as I ran past him at various places throughout the race and then stop it as the next runner ran past him. He would then shout the time-gap as he passed me in the car on his way to the next point. I must stress that at no time here was I interested in setting record times; my concern was solely in beating the other competitors. To be informed that a one-minute gap at 15 miles had grown to three minutes at 19 miles and then to five at 21 miles was a tremendous fillip, especially if I had been tiring. The man behind was obviously worse!

My problem now, if I were to prove my marathon credentials, was that I would have to compete in the British Championship less than a month later as the only road races throughout the remainder of the summer in Scotland were below the full marathon distance. I must admit that I was reluctant to enter as I considered the interval between the Scottish and the AAA (Amateur Athletics Association) marathons far too short to allow for proper recovery. You might think that you were fully fit, but, when the crunch came in those last six miles, you would then begin to think about how much you had taken out of yourself in the previous marathon. Really, it was a psychological problem as much as a physical one. Nevertheless, I had little choice but to travel to Cardiff for the AAA Championship.

Alec Kidd of Garscube Harriers, a cross-country internationalist, who had finished behind me in the Scottish Marathon Championship, went down with me to Wales. To our surprise, neither Duffy, the Scottish champion, nor MacLean, the runner-up were there. It was a nightmare of a race for me, however. Jim Peters set a furious pace – and a new world record! Alec passed me near the end and we finished, I think, in sixth and seventh positions. I was past caring by that time!

Again, I had learned another valuable lesson. Up till then, I had never drunk any liquid in the course of a race. This time, however, I handed in two tiny bottles containing water and glucose to be handed to me at 19 and then 22 miles. After drinking the first at 19 miles, I immediately lost interest in the race and was concerned only with arriving at 22 miles for the second bottle. It certainly did not revive and refresh me. Thereafter, in subsequent races, I abstained completely from drinking any fluids. After all, I had to do so in my long solitary training runs where I had no opportunity of a toilet 'pit-stop' even if I were desperate for one!

The marathon results this year were now posing quite a problem for the officials of the Scottish AAA, who had decided to institute an award, 'The D. McNab Robertson Memorial Trophy', for the best Scottish long-distance road runner anywhere in the world. Eventually, we were told that the leading contenders were Alec Kidd and I, and that the Perth to Dundee race at the end of the season (a distance of 22 miles) would decide the issue.

I led the race for 20 miles and managed to pull away from all the other competitors except the Englishman, Eric Smith. As we approached the Ninewells junction before forking right downhill to the shore road, he asked me how far we had to go. I then proceeded to describe to him at length the last two miles. 'Thanks,' he grunted and completely surprised me by immediately putting in a fast burst and opening up a gap of about 30 yards, which he managed to maintain to the end. It was another salutary lesson for me. I never again wasted unnecessary breath during a race! Both of us, however, had broken last year's Scottish champion Charlie Robertson's record for the course and I had done enough to be awarded, for the first time, the D. McNab Robertson Memorial Trophy, which I was afterwards to win for the next three seasons.

The Scottish Marathon Club's social evening in Glasgow at the end of that summer's season, at which I was presented with the trophy, was to prove an eventful one for me. The guest speaker was the President of the SAAA, Willie Carmichael, who was to be the Scottish Team Manager at the next summer's Empire and Commonwealth Games in Vancouver. An Edinburgh man (head of the city's Lighting and Cleansing Department), Willie issued a couple of challenges to us. There were two longstanding road records, he informed us, the 44 miles Glasgow to Edinburgh and the 23¼ miles from the North Berwick Post Office to the Edinburgh General Post Office. I mentally reserved an attempt on the Glasgow to Edinburgh record until a few years in the future. Alas, injury was later to deny me an opportunity to try it. More immediately, however, I was very interested in the North Berwick to Edinburgh record. This record – 2hrs 38mins 15secs – had stood in the name of J. Morrow since 1929 (the year I was born!) and I knew that it was well within my capabilities. If I could break it convincingly, it would be good publicity for my being considered for selection for next year's Empire and Commonwealth Games when lack of money would again ensure that only a very small team representing all sports would be selected. Accordingly, I contacted Willie Carmichael and set about organising an attempt on the record. I decided that it was not going to be a race against other runners but a solo attempt against the clock – something I had never done before.

My commanding officer at RAF Turnhouse was very co-operative and laid on a truck, driven by one of my fellow officers and our physical training corporal. They made room for my dad and Mr D.A. Jamieson, an official SAAA timekeeper, in the truck. The presidents of both the SAAA (Willie himself) and the National Cross-Country Union of Scotland also acted as recorders. The entourage was completed by press reporters and photographers who had been invited to attend.

After all the arrangements were made for Tuesday, 1 December, disaster struck! Early that morning, the Met Office at Turnhouse informed me that I would be running into a gale-force headwind all the way along the coast from

North Berwick to Edinburgh. I made frantic efforts to contact everyone involved and was exceedingly fortunate to be able to postpone the run till the following Tuesday, 8 December. Then I started praying for good weather as there was no way that I could postpone it a second time. Even if there were a blizzard raging the following week, I would have to go ahead with it!

Fortunately, the weather was almost perfect as I started out at noon from the Post Office in the centre of North Berwick – bright but cold. There was a slight facing wind and later a scattering of raindrops. I started fast and ran at a very even pace. Though my breathing was smooth, my calf muscles began to feel sore at five miles. Perhaps foolishly, I had capped off my previous week's training with a decidedly long, fairly easy 27-mile run on the Saturday (2hrs 56mins 52secs), and on the Sunday and Monday my legs were still rather sore. However, I maintained my pace and the stiffness gradually wore off.

The route hugged the coast through Dirleton, Gullane, Aberlady, Port Seton, Prestonpans, Levenhall, Musselburgh and Joppa and then right along Portobello High Street. My time for the 20-plus miles to Portobello – 1hr 49mins 5secs – was fast. Indeed, my fastest stretch was from 16 to 20 miles. The hills over the last three miles, however, slowed my speed a little – especially from Meadowbank Stadium up London Road and along the left side of Calton Hill with the roofs of Holyrood Palace away below me to the left. The last quarter of a mile, thankfully, was downhill past the Scottish Office to Princes Street, and I put on a spurt, finishing fast – and fresh with something still in hand – in a time of 2hrs 5mins 19secs. I had succeeded far beyond my expectations, having knocked almost 33 minutes off the previous record! I had achieved, too, my main aim in attracting publicity. One of the newspapers, indeed, quoted

Willie Carmichael referring to me at the finishing point as 'a future Dunky Wright' (Scotland's previous Empire Games Marathon winner).

I knew now that I was marathon-fit and that I had a real chance of the Scottish Marathon title if I could maintain and improve my training and, above all, stay injury-free during the next five months. The key date for me in the 1954 season was Saturday, 29 May. The SAAA Marathon Championship had been brought forward this year to give as long an interval as possible before the Empire and Commonwealth Games began at the end of July.

I faced one major problem, however: within the next three months, I would have to compete in a fairly hectic programme of important cross-country races for both the RAF and my club, Shettleston Harriers. These would include the Scottish Inter-District race and International Trial, the Midland District Championship, the RAF Northern Area Championship, the RAF Finals Championship, the Inter-Services Championship, the Scottish NCCU Championship and possibly the International (12 Nations) Championship. My training, however, would need to be all on the road and over much longer distances. The obvious drawbacks would be the constant interruption to my marathon preparation before each of these races, the psychological reaction after being keyed-up each time and the very real danger of injury over the different terrain.

The obvious and sensible course would have been to avoid the cross-country programme completely and to concentrate single-mindedly on my road training. However, my loyalty and duty to the RAF and my club – and my own ambition – effectively precluded that option. Indeed, I really wanted to win a third-in-a-row Inter-Services Championship medal and also my first Scottish international cross-country vest, which the exigencies of my RAF service had prevented me from competing for during the previous two seasons.

It would be best if I described these vital five months before my marathon test under three headings: Training, Cross-Country Races and Injury Problems.

Training

I took the risk and compromised. I decided to maintain my full programme of marathon training and treat each cross-country race not as an objective in itself but simply as part of my mileage programme, with no pre-race easing-off days and trying not to become emotionally keyed-up prior to nor disappointed perhaps after each race. If injury or health problems arose, I would as far as possible ignore them, easing off, perhaps, the speed and distance of my runs but trying to maintain my daily stint. For example, at the end of that year, 1953, I injured my back running 12 miles on Christmas Day, but, despite the soreness, I ran 18½ miles next day, rested on the Sunday, managed 12 miles on the Monday, rested again on the Tuesday, and then tackled a double run on the Wednesday, 12 miles in the morning and 10½ in the afternoon. On Hogmanay, I again ran 12 miles and then, on New Year's Day, I managed over 30 miles. Next day, I ran 5½ in the morning and still managed a fierce ten miles in fast bursts over the country with Eddie Bannon, the Scottish cross-country champion, in the afternoon. Thus, in spite of injury forcing two rest-days that week, I nevertheless managed a total of 92 miles for the remainder of the week and my recovery was complete. Incidentally, my 30-plus miler on New Year's Day became a tradition with me. I felt that, if I were able to run over 30 miles then in the middle of winter, I would be able to race the marathon distance in the summer.

Influenced to some extent by Arthur Newton, the famous South African professional, I was a firm believer in the value of long easy runs. My marathon predecessors in Scotland used to walk 30-odd miles on a Sunday, but that took them all day! I really did not have the time to spare, so I decided to run long distances instead. I was a section commander in the RAF and had to fit my training into my work pattern. I therefore tried to manage a very long run on the Sunday and another on the Wednesday sports afternoon. By cutting out lunch in the officers' mess I was able to run 20-plus miles (at times even up to 32¼) from Edinburgh (Turnhouse) back to my home in Falkirk and still have the better part of the afternoon free, having saved both time and bus fare! On other days, I tried to fit in 15 miles during my extended lunch breaks. Locking myself into my office afterwards, sandwich in hand and often clad only in a towel, I would answer the phone, safe in the knowledge that, as my section-office was on the perimeter of the airfield, my superiors would not drop in unannounced!

In these five months, therefore, I ran 12 times over 25 miles (twice 32¼ miles) as well as several 20-plus milers. Sometimes, I also did 5½ miles in the morning and 20-plus in the afternoon or evening of the same day. My weekly mileage was certainly boosted by these long runs: for example, for the third week of March (the most hectic month for cross-country championships) I clocked 121 miles, for the second week in April 112 miles and for the third week in May (the week before my vital marathon championship) 117½ miles.

Cross-Country Races

My results in the cross-country championships in these first three months of this year were mixed but I succeeded in my main aims and was relatively pleased with my success. On Saturday, 9 January, I finished second to Eddie Bannon in the Seven Miles International Trial and Inter-District race run over a three-lap course at Shettleston. Last at the start, I speeded up too fast into fifth place at the end of the first lap and suffered stomach pains on my slow second lap, but, surprisingly, in view of the heavy ploughs and two burns to jump, I managed a storming finish to record the fastest last lap of 10mins 52secs and an overall time of 32mins 38secs. I learned one vital lesson that day: I found that I was at a distinct disadvantage wearing cross-country shoes with rubber studs, which rapidly clogged up with mud and grass and, on the advice of Allan Scally, the Shettleston Harriers coach, I decided to wear spikes over the country from then on even when short stretches of road had to be negotiated!

My next race, on 6 February, the Midland District Championship at Lenzie, was a setback. I finished fourth behind runners (Harry Fenion and Tommy Tracey) whom I had beaten in my last race. No doubt, I was still suffering from the debilitating effect of a bout of severe sickness brought on by a stomach chill after drinking a pint of milk with my sandwiches on the Monday of this week. Nevertheless, I had again started too slowly and never made contact with the leaders over a very heavy, muddy course. I was very bad, too, at negotiating the fences, cutting my knee when I tried to hurdle one and my spikes caught on the wire as I tried to imitate Bellahouston's Bob Climie, a six-foot Glasgow policeman and a steeplechaser of note running beside me. Equally disastrous was my attempt to go under another fence when I had to rip myself off the barbed wire, tearing my singlet and scarring my back in the process. Oh the joys of cross-country running!

I redeemed myself, however, on the following Wednesday, 10 February, when I won the RAF Northern

Area Seven Miles Championship at Dishforth in Yorkshire. This race should have been run the previous week, Wednesday, 3 February, when I was so sick the night before travelling, but, fortunately for me, it was postponed on account of snowstorms. The conditions, however, were equally appalling this week also (six inches of snow) and the event was about to be postponed for a second time. Meeting the organisers in the officers' mess, however, I suggested putting a bulldozer round the airfield perimeter track and holding the race over two laps. Frank Scally, my Shettleston Harriers clubmate, and I then decided to follow his dad's advice and wear spikes on the resulting hard-packed snow and ice-covered road. The start was very fast and I ran well back before taking the lead after approximately 2¾ miles. Thereafter, I was out on my own and, though the going was extremely slippy, I won by almost 300 yards. Frank ran his best-ever race to finish second, ahead of Pat Ranger, the RAF champion and English internationalist, who was to finish third in the International Cross-Country Championship.

My next race, the RAF Finals at RAF Benson, near Reading, the following Wednesday, 17 February, was especially important for me. If I were to achieve my hopes for three successive Inter-Services Championship medals, I had to finish in the first eight to be selected for the RAF team. This race stands out in my mind as it involved one of the most bizarre incidents I ever encountered in my running career.

As should be clear by now, I was not naturally a fast starter and I frequently suffered in the mad, jostling rush at the start of the big cross-country events. In my earlier years, I had discovered to my cost the folly of attempting to run at my own even pace from the gun and ignoring the leaders who always set out at sprinting speed to get clear of the melee before settling down. Time and again I had been left so far behind that, by the time I had won through the mob of slower runners, the fast men had established an uncatchable lead. I had, therefore, evolved my own technique of starting as evenly as possible, letting myself be carried along in the pack and avoiding trouble for the first half-mile; then I would suddenly explode into my own sprint at the very moment that the others had expended their initial surge. I had found to my gratification that this burst usually took me right through the throng and on to the heels of the leaders. Then I was able to hang on to their pace, simply ignoring the distance ahead until my breathing gradually settled down into the rhythm of my own racing speed. On some occasions, indeed, my gamble had been so successful that I had found myself sustaining my burst right past the leaders and establishing a clear gap, which I had managed not only to keep but even to increase to the finish – notably my win from a big field in the Midland Area RAF Championship at Cranwell in the spring of 1952.

Today, as usual, I was left very badly at the start. My thighs were sore and stiff over the first heavy fields and I had a very tough fight to get through the mob. Still, I began my fast burst. Ahead of me, two six-footers were running together along a narrow lane before the top of a ploughed field. The gap between them was narrow and, just as I headed for it, it narrowed still further. I burst between them like a cork out of a bottle, gasping an apology as I bumped them. A yelled expletive came in reply from behind me as I continued my burst. Then suddenly I felt my shoulders gripped and the next thing I knew I was hurtling downhill into the muddy plough. The taller, a redhead, had stopped after expending his remaining energies to catch me up. I jumped up, fists raised instinctively, but, before I could do anything disastrous, I heard a warning shout, 'Sir, sir, forget it!' It was a sergeant in the Medical Branch in London, who had represented the RAF with me in previous Inter-Services Championships. I came to my senses. We had gone about a mile and a half and I had still five miles to try to win my place in the RAF team. It was a gruelling battle. I disliked intensely the very heavy going, but I managed to finish in seventh place, easing up and looking round, my place in the team secured for the third time.

Afterwards, as I walked through the milling crowds of competitors back to the changing rooms, I suddenly spotted my attacker. I immediately walked up to him and said, 'I've never encountered such behaviour in our sport!' Covered in mud as I was, something in my tone, however, must have alerted him that I carried rank, for he only muttered back in a broad Glasgow accent (though he was representing a Welsh team, RAF St Athan) that it was the last b… time he would run cross-country.

The incident was not finished, however. The Medical Branch sergeant then caught me and asked what further action I was proposing to take. I told him that the matter was ended as far as I was concerned. I didn't even know who the man was. He replied that he did. He had stopped during the race and noted the man's number! I finally had to go to the Air Commodore, the officer in charge of the race, and tell him that, if any complaint was made on my behalf, I wanted the matter dropped.

Three days later, I had recovered sufficiently to finish second to Eddie Bannon in the Shettleston Harriers Championship, but two weeks afterwards (6 March) came my most important test if I were to be selected for the national team – namely the Nine Miles Scottish National Championship on Hamilton racecourse. Finishing seventh, I did in fact win my international vest, but I was still somewhat disappointed. Though I had been suffering from a bad chesty cold and though the going was heavy on the turf and the very muddy loops into the surrounding countryside, I should still have done better as Tracey, Fenion, Kane and McKenzie, all of whom I had beaten in January, finished ahead of me. One consolation, however, was that we (Shettleston Harriers) won the team championship.

The Scottish team travelled down to Birmingham on Thursday, 25 March. My back stiffened badly on the train en route, but that evening I joined in a six-mile training run from Birchfield Harriers' ground, paced by Bobby Reid of Birchfield. The following day, we jogged slowly over two laps of the international course at Bromford Bridge racecourse and, though my stiffness had now subsided, my back was massaged that evening by the trainer.

The Nine Miles International Championship, run over four laps of the racecourse, however, turned out to be a bad race for me. I finished 50th, seventh Scot, and nearly all of the Scots ahead of me I had beaten earlier in the season. I blundered badly by ignoring my usual plan for starting. Carried away by the excitement of the occasion, I started very fast and, with three other Scots, I was in the first six when we turned off the racecourse after 350 yards. I soon fell back rapidly, my stomach troubling and, though running more strongly towards the end, I could only recover from ninth place in the team to seventh. Even more than in previous cross-country races, I found that I was running very uncomfortably over the very rough, uneven grassland and I was forced to conclude that my road training was really very unsuitable for such heavy going.

One disappointing feature of this, my first international trip, was the ignoring of the athletes by the Scots team official party when it came to the entertainment laid on by the Birmingham organisers. The main item was a tour to Stratford-on-Avon. When I asked our officials why we had not been told of it, I was informed that they did not think that we would be interested in Shakespeare! I pointed out that I was a qualified English teacher (MA Hons. English Language and Literature) but it was all too late. Similar treatment of the athletes was to occur on my later cross-country international trips to Spain and Portugal.

To make matters worse for me, after returning to Scotland from this rather exhausting race, I had, only two days later, to travel to Portsmouth for the Six Miles Inter-Services Cross-Country Championship at HMS *Dryad*, Southwick. However, I was much better pleased with my performance here. Despite the going underfoot being heavy and muddy, I finished eighth and, in the sixth counting position for the RAF, I had won my third Inter-Services Championship medal in a row after all! I started slowly this time and gradually worked my way through the field but went off the course twice (not an unknown happening for me!), losing over 50 yards and two places to the Army and Navy. Though I passed them again a quarter of a mile from the end, Humphries, the Navy champion, passed me once more on the last 80 yards but I hauled out my best-ever finish to catch him 20 yards from the tape. I must say I felt much better and easier than on the previous Saturday in Birmingham! A hat-trick of wins for the RAF was certainly a great achievement. That these championship races against the other services were occasions of great rivalry had been brought home to me on my first competing in them in 1952 at the Army camp at Blandford in Dorset. I was jogging down a grassy slope towards the start when one of the spectators called out peremptorily, 'McGhee!' Turning, I saw from his raincoat that he was an RAF officer. Then I recognised him – Group Captain Don Finlay, the famous Olympic hurdler! 'Get back uphill again,' he ordered, 'and collect the RAF boys. Wait until the Army and Navy runners are on the starting line. Then come down smartly as a team.'

My last race of that winter season before my marathon test at the end of May 1954 meant another trip to London with Shettleston Harriers the following week (10 April). The London to Brighton Road Relay was much more to my liking. Running the third lap (5 miles 1,416 yards) from Mitcham to Purley Rise (past Croydon Airport), I recorded a time of 29mins 9secs, one of the fastest for this lap. Taking over in eighth place, I was passed just after the handover by Peter Pirie (brother of the more famous Gordon) but managed to haul in another two places before handing over the baton in seventh position. Unfortunately, Frank Scally collapsed on the ninth lap and the team was disqualified. I was pleased, however, that I had survived the winter cross-country season without too much serious interruption to my marathon preparation.

Injury Problems

There still remained the fear of injury, however. In discussing my training earlier, I said that my policy was as far as possible to ignore injuries or illness by easing off the speed and distance of my runs and attempting to run off the problem. I threw off, for example, my back injury at Christmas and its reoccurrence just prior to the Birmingham International in March, my Achilles tendon trouble in the third week of January and my knee injury at the end of that month, though each of them were to recur with greater severity in later years; indeed, the back and finally the knee problems eventually put an end to my athletic career.

This year, however, the really serious problem with my left Achilles tendon began on Tuesday, 13 April, only a couple of days after my return from the London to Brighton Relay race, but, as usual, I tried to run it off. I even ran a 25-miler on the Thursday of that week. I ran every day and even twice on the Saturday. My training notes commented that the pain was wearing off as I warmed up into my runs but, more ominously, that it was returning again after I finished. On the Sunday I was forced to rest and decided (wisely as it was to prove) not to risk travelling to Doncaster for the Doncaster to Sheffield Marathon on Easter Monday. On the Tuesday I ran a slow 12 miles in the morning but, when I tried to run slowly again in the evening, the ankle was very painful all the time and I could manage only two miles. Something drastic had to be done and the following day I succeeded in getting an appointment with T. McClurg Anderson at his private practice in the West End of Glasgow.

I had first met McClurg Anderson on a memorable trip to Ireland when I was 17 and in my first year at Glasgow University, where he acted as physiotherapist and coach to the athletics team. I had finished third in the mile in Belfast, managing to beat my older team-mate, the later world-famous psychiatrist, R.D. Laing. My first place in the last event of the evening, the three miles, at Trinity College, Dublin, ahead of my team-mate Major (later the Rev.) David Johnstone, had won the meeting for Glasgow by a single point. I was pretty certain that Tom Anderson would remember me now, seven years later.

He diagnosed a torn tendon, strapped up my ankle and advised immediate rest and the old-fashioned hot-salt treatment, which Allan Scally, my coach, was also to use on and off with me in the years ahead. It consisted of heating coarse rock salt crystals in a pan until they were sparking and pouring them into a sock, which was then moulded round the affected part. I followed his advice and, on Saturday, 24 April, he also gave me diathermy treatment. I rested the ankle all the following week (my longest spell without a run for quite some time) and was treated again at Anderson's house on Saturday, 1 May, when he advised me to attempt to run no more than one mile at a time in easy stages with my ankle strapped up on each occasion.

The Scottish Marathon Championship, however, was only four weeks away, so I decided to ignore most of Anderson's advice and next day I tried a slow 2½-mile run. On the Monday, I ran 3½, on Tuesday 5½, on Wednesday 5½ and 10 in the evening, on Thursday 10 and 5½ in the evening, 10 again on Friday and 5½ on Saturday morning. Every day I undertook heat treatment at RAF Turnhouse and then the hot-salt application at home in the evening. By the end of that week, I was running easily and only felt the ankle when walking upstairs in the evening. On the Saturday, I met Tom Anderson and his assistant, Mr Kinloch. They treated my leg again and were astonished that I had managed to run 58 miles that week. Afterwards, I went to the start of the Anniesland to Vale of Leven 15 Miles Road Race. Of course, there was no possibility of my being able to compete, but I decided to follow the progress of the race in the vehicle carrying the competitors' clothes. I soon realised that the winner, Willie Gallacher, now a clubmate of mine at Shettleston and King of Greenock, the runner-up, would be formidable contenders in the marathon in three weeks' time.

The following week, I threw caution to the winds and, despite my leg still troubling on and off, I put in nine training sessions totalling 98½ miles, including 21½ miles on my Wednesday afternoon run. I did another 21½ miles over a different route on the following Sunday and managed a 28¼-miler on the next Wednesday with my tendon only slightly sore and weak at the end. This last full week before the marathon, I totalled 117½ miles in nine sessions. I was reasonably sure that I had overcome this last bout of serious injury just in time!

The SAAA Marathon Championship 1954

Saturday, 29 May, the SAAA Marathon Championship, was fast approaching. This year, it was to be run over an entirely new course – from the far side of the Cloch Lighthouse beyond Gourock and then right along the Clyde estuary through Gourock, Greenock and Renfrew to Rangers' Ibrox Stadium, where it would be a closing highlight of the Glasgow Highland Gathering.

I always believed in knowing just exactly what the last miles of any race were like, so on the Saturday before the race I decided to travel to Renfrew, where I changed at the King George V Playing Fields. I then ran over the closing miles of the marathon course to Ibrox and back and continued on to Inchinnan before returning to the changing rooms (11¼ miles in all). I saw clearly that all would depend on the weather conditions the following week. On such an open course, a wind would be an asset if it were blowing at our backs but a very serious disadvantage if it were in our faces – as, unfortunately, it was the following week!

Just before we started, Dunky Wright announced that he would do his best to ensure that the winner was selected for the Scottish team for the Vancouver Games. I estimated that my toughest rivals among the 29 starters would be Duffy, last year's champion, Gallacher (Vale of Leven), King (Greenock), the veteran Farrell (Maryhill), Campbell (Fort William), the Ben Nevis winner, and, above all, the dark horse, Laurence (Teviotdale). The latter and I had never met, but he had been undefeated in road races in the Borders and the east earlier in the season.

It was a warm bright day, but, alas, there was an adverse easterly wind that was to last all the way and, indeed, become stronger, especially over the last two or three miles. The start was fast, I immediately tucked in behind Laurence, using him as a shield when the wind gusted badly, and by two miles (covered in 11mins 3secs), the pattern of the race was set with Laurence, Duffy and I the leading group. We passed the five-mile mark in 27mins 11secs and at ten miles (56mins 27secs) I found myself momentarily in the lead, with Laurence a step behind. (Duffy and King were now 26 seconds behind.) The two of us ran elbow to elbow to 12 miles (66mins 34secs), with Gallacher now in third place, 52 seconds behind, but for a spell over the next mile I was 'hanging on' behind Laurence's shoulder. Indeed, I had never forced the pace at all in the race so far. I gradually recovered, however, and, seeing the photographers focusing on the 15-mile mark, which we passed in 1hr 24mins 21secs, vanity drove me past Laurence. It is strange how such a triviality could change the entire fortunes of the race. To my astonishment, I sensed a gap opening and was told a quarter of a mile later that he had retired. I was now completely on my own, though still slightly less than a minute ahead of Gallacher. Exhilaration that my closest rival had gone enabled me to increase my speed and I ran my fastest three miles to 18 miles.

I was still worried, however, about how far the others were behind but I dared not look back in case I gave encouragement to them. I was missing my dad for regular updates on the gap but, unfortunately, we had not been able to arrange transport for him that day. Then came a shout out of the blue. A friend and former Glasgow University classmate of mine, Jack Gaskell, had unexpectedly appeared on a powerful motorcycle. My problem was solved: he could now provide me with the information I needed!

The wind was worsening, however, and I felt it bad at 20 miles, which I reached in 1hr 54mins 57secs. I was slowing but, to my relief, Gallacher was falling farther behind (over three minutes now) and, indeed, he retired at 21 miles. I was told that Duffy had dropped out at 17 miles, so with my closest rivals all gone and the others falling farther and farther behind, my battle was now with myself over the closing miles. I recovered and ran strongly to between 23 and 24 miles, where the wind again increased over the last two miles. The sight of the stadium, however, revived me completely and I finished very powerfully round the track for my first-ever full-distance marathon win. At the age of 24, too, I had become the youngest winner of the Scottish Marathon title.

The Chieftain of the Gathering then crowned me with the traditional laurel wreath – a small one, Nero-like round my brow, unlike the larger ones round my shoulders that I was to receive in subsequent years – and, thus attired, I ran another lap of honour round the Ibrox track. I was even more exhilarated when I learned that my time, despite the wind, was a new Scottish record – 2hrs 35mins 22secs. The second finisher was Emmet Farrell in 2hrs 43mins 8secs, with King third in 2hrs 47mins 4secs. Now I could only await the deliberations of the selection committee.

Next day, reaction set in: I had to force myself out into training again – despite my legs being very stiff and sore and stitching badly after two miles. Before I had completed my six-mile run, however, I was again running more easily and, indeed, that week I completed 94½ miles.

I had one major problem facing me, however: I had promised to compete in the Dundee half-marathon at the inauguration of the new Caird Park Stadium at the end of the week and I knew that a bad performance could seriously jeopardise my chances of Empire Games selection. Indeed, I almost regretted my decision to risk competing when, as I was completing a half-mile warm-up, I saw Charlie Robertson on the starting line. The 1952 Scottish Marathon champion had not competed in last week's race and would be much fresher!

It was a dull, coldish day for June and a stiff easterly wind was blowing. Nevertheless, I decided on a very fast start and led throughout the initial two laps of the track. Out on the road, I rapidly increased my lead. My calf muscles were sore but I kept 'hammering it' over both road laps. In spite of the steep hill up to the Kingsway on each lap, I managed to keep up the pace and finished very fast on the track in 1hr 7mins 42secs. To my astonishment, I found that I was over a mile ahead of Charlie, who finished second in 1hr 13mins 2secs. My gamble had paid off. I felt that I was still on course for Empire Games selection.

On one matter, however, I was adamant. There was now no way in which I would be inveigled into a track race and risk messing up my legs. Running tracks in those days could not be compared with the beautifully smooth modern surfaces. They were either loose and ashy cinder tracks (often rutted into the bargain!) or simply grass (sometimes not too short and frequently very heavy indeed). The latter was the case at our previous year's RAF Turnhouse sports when the 440-yard track was simply measured out round the rugby pitch. I was ordered to represent Station Headquarters in the inter-section competition. Reluctantly I agreed to run but only in the three miles. Without risking spikes I decided just to wear my usual gym shoes, which I used in my training on the roads. Two runners from each section lined up and my team-mate, my corporal clerk, volunteered to take the lead and asked me to tuck in behind him. The pace of that first lap, however, was so funereal that I lost patience. I was certainly not going to run at what I considered an easy jog for 11 laps as the field obviously intended and then risk a mad sprint for the last lap. I therefore shot into the lead and broke completely from the rest. I kept piling on the pace and, indeed, won by over half a mile, having lapped everyone twice. My time, especially in view of that very slow first lap, was quite respectable – 15mins 3secs. In fact, I then realised that I could quite easily have won the mile and probably the half-mile as well! The CO was so impressed that, at our next weekly section commanders' meeting, he instructed the physical fitness officer to send my time to Fighter Command's headquarters. Privately, however, I asked him to send my marathon time instead and, for weeks afterwards, the CO kept wondering why I was not hearing about my selection for the RAF representative track teams. I certainly had no ambitions in that direction and was only too glad that this, one of my rare track races, had not resulted in possible injury and damage to my marathon prospects.

Nevertheless, I yet had to keep up a fairly strenuous road training schedule and do my RAF work at the same time. Despite having to travel to Nottinghamshire for a spell on Fighter Command's examination marking board, I managed over the next three weeks to fit in 119, 107 and 113 miles, including a 28¼ mile run and a 27-miler, each in just over three hours.

Then came the great news that I had been selected for the Scottish team. I was later told that it had been a close-run thing. Each sport's governing body had put up a tough fight for their nominees and I had been voted in last member of the 21! The athletics contingent, indeed, mustered only four men and one woman (Pat Devine, our sprint champion). The clinching argument in my favour, apparently, seemed to have been based on the grounds of advertising rather than on realistic hopes of a medal: the comment was that, with me, the Scottish colours would be carried for over two hours round the streets of Vancouver, whereas a sprinter might be seen for only about ten seconds!

My elation, however, was soon dampened by fears about my fitness. On one of my training runs on the Newark to Leicester road during the marking board at RAF Newton, I had felt the first twinges of the Achilles tendon trouble that was later to worry me so much in Vancouver, but also, and more worryingly, pains in my lower right side, which, at the time, I put down to having to adhere to the service meal times (and menus!) and to fitting in my training at irregular hours. On my return to Edinburgh the following week, I ran a 25-miler on Sunday, 27 June, despite both intermittent ankle and side pains, but could manage only 5½ miles at Turnhouse on the Monday owing to the pains in my lower right side and groin. I ran no more that week but was then forced to seek medical advice. My fear, obviously, was of appendicitis. My GP, Dr Brannan, soon reassured me. 'If it had been appendicitis,' he grinned, as he tapped and prodded, 'when I hit you there, you would have hit the roof!' His diagnosis was simply indigestion plus a slight groin strain and he prescribed a bottle of stomach medicine, which I was to take for the next week. I shall never forget my overwhelming feeling of relief as I walked away from his surgery that evening. Then, despite slight pains on and off from both side and ankle, I immediately got back into training and managed to log 98 miles that following week and almost 108 the week after.

I had then only two days left before the flight to Canada and I ran 16 miles on both the Sunday and Monday. On the evening before departure, the Falkirk

Windsor Road Gala Day Committee invited me to their meeting in their 'Hut', where I was surprised to see so many of my friends and neighbours. My dad stood down as chairman for the evening and I was welcomed by Tom Aird, the acting chairman, Walter Murison, the treasurer, and Tommy Myles, the secretary. After Mrs G. McPhie presented me with a large iron horseshoe decked in tartan, our close neighbour, Mr J. Young, spoke glowingly about the progress of 'Our Joe'. Thanking them all for their best wishes, I promised to wear the tartan ribbon pinned to my shorts during the race, but obviously the horseshoe was too heavy to carry in my luggage! I was then rather embarrassed when they all escorted me home, led by piper Harry Treeby, to the tune of 'Scotland the Brave'. Little did I anticipate then, however, the scale of the welcome they were to give me on my return.

Next day, Tuesday, 20 July, the Scottish team departed at 2pm from Prestwick airport, where I was seen off by my closest supporters – my mum, dad and sister Louise, and my mentors, Joe Walker, who had started me running at St Modan's High School, Stirling, and Allan Scally, the Shettleston Harriers coach. Unfortunately, my brother Charlie was on RAF service in England and could not get leave. I was ignored, however, by the waiting press – unlike the morning of my return to Prestwick almost four weeks later.

The flight on the Trans-Canadian Airlines plane with the Welsh team and some of the English was in two stages. The first to Montreal was uneventful and wearisome and took 13 hours before we touched down at 3am our time (10pm Montreal). I slept rather fitfully that night in the somewhat cramped airport hotel, being awakened from time to time by the haunting and alien hooting of a train in the far distance. Next day, our flight left at 10am for

Vancouver. My seat was to the front of the plane and I have vivid memories of passing over the lakes and apparently limitless prairies until lowering clouds over the Rocky Mountains ahead presaged a storm, which duly hit us with some force. The sickening and sudden lurches and drops in height were, to say the least, alarming and I was certainly glad when we left the storm behind and touched down at Vancouver airport. The flight had taken us seven hours, but again we had to set our watches back as it was only 3pm there.

Our Canadian hosts gave us a hearty welcome but later expressed disappointment that we were indistinguishable in our white Panama hats, dark blue blazers and flannels from our fellow Britons. They had expected us in kilts! I remember, indeed, one of our enthusiastic Scots-Canadian hosts later asking me if we would have worn kilts supplied by them. My amused reply 'yes' was abruptly cut short by Willie Carmichael's irascible interjection: 'Certainly not! The kilt is not the dress of the Lowland Scot!' A cavalcade of cars, horns hooting, then paraded us through the city at rush hour to the Empire Village, a permanently hutted encampment, destined later for student accommodation, on the University of British Columbia campus.

Chapter 2

Canada: The Build-up to the Race

AFTER TEA and then leisurely unpacking in the room I was to share with Ron Parks, our sole cycling representative, I decided to set out on a short run to loosen up after so many hours' confinement in the planes over the last two days.

Passing the Mountie on guard at the gate of the Village, I met another marathon runner with the same idea as myself – Les Stokell from Victoria – and we chatted as we ran at a leisurely pace, he in his red Canadian tracksuit top and I in my royal blue with 'Scotland' emblazoned across the back. The evening air was cool and exhilarating as we trotted along beneath the shade of huge evergreen trees. Suddenly I spotted an opening on my left leading into a grove dominated by a semi-circle of tall totem poles. As we stopped to admire the awesome spectacle of these carved effigies of eagle and bear, a feeling of alienation, the sense of being in a foreign land, struck me forcibly. It was dispelled a few moments later as we resumed our run.

The traffic on the road was fairly light, but one car containing a family of sightseers sat on our heels before cruising very slowly past us with the driver loudly intoning,

'You are doing exactly ten miles an hour.' The following car behaved even more oddly. As it slewed across the road, the driver stuck his head out of the window and, addressing me specifically, asked in a Canadian accent for directions to the Empire Village. I should have suspected his ploy at once, as Les, the Canadian and practically a local, was the obvious man to ask. Nevertheless, I laboriously tried to tell him that he was heading in the wrong direction and that the Village lay behind us. He at once laughed delightedly and then shouted, 'Guid auld Glesca!' before tooting his horn and driving off.

The following morning, a brilliantly sunny one, I got down to serious training again. First, however, we had to attend in full formal dress uniform a photo-call and a short flag-raising ceremony welcoming the Scottish team to the village. There were grins all round as they played a record of the then Scottish anthem, 'Scots Wha Hae', at double the normal speed!

Afterwards, I quickly changed, ran the few miles to the main stadium to view it briefly and then continued through the suburban streets for a total of 21 miles, which was to be my longest pre-race run. In the last few miles, disaster struck: my left Achilles tendon, which had troubled me earlier that year, suddenly began to ache. I knew that the only real cure would be rest. I had already fixed up, however, with Dr Douglas, our team captain, and Colonel Usher, the fencing official from Edinburgh University, to go over the marathon course by car the next day, and, rather foolishly, I got out of the car and ran fairly smartly, though in pain, for 12 miles. On the Saturday morning, I again ran 12 miles but much more slowly this time. Indeed, despite our long flights on Tuesday and Wednesday, I found that I had logged 83 miles since the previous Sunday.

I was determined to continue training – no matter how short or how slow the runs might be. On the Sunday, the Australian swimming coach strapped up my ankle. I then wore this strapping on and off for the next week and managed to keep running every day, totalling 64 miles for this week (the shortest run only half a mile on the Tuesday). Twice, however, my pride had nearly caused further aggravation of the injury. On the Monday, I forced myself to keep up with Stan Cox's fast pace from 10 to 19 miles of the course with Jim Peters watching us in the accompanying car for a mile before joining in, and, on the Friday, I ran fast over the last 11 miles of the course as Willie Carmichael, my team manager, was watching from the car. The pain did not worsen, however, and, though it still bothered me during every single run of the third week, I managed 47 miles in total for the six days before the race on the Saturday (the last day only one mile). The astonishing thing, however, was that I completely forgot about the ankle during the race and, indeed, in all my races thereafter!

Perhaps the cause was partly psychological and Colonel Usher was more correct than I realised. He had decided one day to give me massage treatment. Carefully explaining that he was about to transmit the energy from his fingertips into my ankle, he proceeded to strip to the waist and take a series of deep breaths before pounding away at the tendon. Apprehensive of incurring further injury, I hastily assured him that it now felt much better. He rather sabotaged his own efforts a few minutes later when I overheard his remark to a bystander that 'it won't do him a damn bit good, but he thinks it does'!

When I look back on it, I realise now that this Achilles tendon trouble was really a blessing in disguise, especially when we remember how hot the weather was. It forced me to take much slower and shorter runs, thus conserving my energies for the race itself.

Psychologically, too, there was another benefit. Thinking that I had now lost whatever slight chance of success I might have hoped for, I decided to make the most of my stay in Vancouver. It would be a once-in-a-lifetime experience. I resolved to accept every invitation and to attend every function and sightseeing trip I possibly could. If our swimmers or boxers, for example, were invited out for an evening, I would join them. After our post-war austerity at home, the millionaire-style way of life in some of these private homes was an eye-opener.

Moreover, when the actual competitions started, I am sure I saw more of the different sports than anyone else in our team did. My identity card, No. 697 (my race number as well) entitled me to 'all the privileges and facilities arranged for visitors'. These included free entry to cinemas (I saw one of the first showings of *Three Coins in a Fountain*) and travel on public transport. The latter was scarcely needed, however, as there was a splendid system of volunteer drivers who were prepared to take you in their own cars all over the city. I was even ferried to the home of a family formerly from the Falkirk area, who had left a message for me at the Village. The identity cards also allowed all competitors into the main stadium, no matter which sport they represented, and into the venues for their own particular sports. As an athlete, however, I was allowed only into the main stadium. Therefore, I became a swimmer or a boxer and, carrying one of their bags, bluffed my way in with our teams when they were competing. I even managed to get into the weightlifting venue and thoroughly enjoyed my evening.

As a Scot, moreover, I felt even more privileged than competitors from other countries. The Scottish team, indeed, were singled out for special attention and received more invitations than we could possibly accept. My diary, for example, lists the following events, which I attended in the eight days prior to the Opening Ceremony:

> Thursday, 22 July: Dinner at the Royal Yacht Club
>
> Friday, 23 July: *Brigadoon* at The Theatre Under the Stars
>
> Saturday, 24 July: The Caledonian Games (far more traditionally Scottish than any Highland Games in which I have competed in Scotland!) and in the evening a visit to British Properties
>
> Sunday, 25 July: Cruise to Bowen Island on the Lieutenant Governor of British Columbia's yacht (competitors from other countries had to use the public cruiser)
>
> Monday, 26 July: Visit to the Lynchs (a Falkirk family)
>
> Tuesday, 27 July: Evening rehearsal for Opening Ceremony
>
> Wednesday, 28 July: Dinner at the Jessimans, North Vancouver (with the swimmers and officials)
>
> Thursday, 29 July: Chairlift up Grouse Mountain; visit to Capilano Suspension Bridge; and visit from the Liddles (another Falkirk family)

All these events were enjoyable but two in particular stick in my mind: our Friday evening at the open-air theatre and the following Sunday's visit to Bowen Island. The musical, *Brigadoon*, was memorable both from the Canadians' enthusiasm for all things Scottish and the humorously embarrassing predicament of some of our group. We ought to have realised that, though the daytime temperatures were high, the evenings could be decidedly chilly – especially in an open-air theatre! The men in our party did not particularly feel the cold as we were wearing our heavy sweaters and blazers. The girl swimmers, however, had come in light summer dresses and they soon started shivering after darkness fell. The male swimmers (all very big men) passed over their sweaters during the first act. At the interval, we were taken aback when spotlights focussed on our row and the manager asked the Scottish team to stand. The applause dissolved into laughter as the girls rose, engulfed in enormous sweaters to their knees and with sleeves flopping well over their hands.

The yacht trip, however, gave me a bit of a fright. Arriving at the island, we anchored about 100 yards from the landing stage and the swimmers in our group, already changed, promptly dived overboard and swam across to the land. Rather foolishly, I decided to follow them. I jumped into the water and began a cautious breaststroke. Reaching about halfway, however, I began to tire and, seeing the shore apparently still so far away, I panicked, turned around and headed slowly back to the ship. I was extremely glad to clutch at a ladder and haul myself painfully up. I resolved then to avoid any exercise other than running before I competed!

On more formal occasions, I volunteered to represent the Scottish competitors; for example, the meeting with Lord Alexander, the Canadian Club lunch with the Duke of Edinburgh and also an evening dinner attended by the Duke. The only time Willie Carmichael did not allow me to leave the Village was the Friday evening before my race, when I could watch our boxers' finals only on television. Almost all my time in these weeks of waiting, indeed, was occupied to the full, but all these activities had served the valuable purpose of preventing my brooding over what might happen in my own event. That night, however, I began to feel the familiar pre-race tension.

Saturday Morning, 7 August 1954

After a restless and fitful sleep, I woke up next morning to find my worst fears realised. Willie Carmichael had been right in his predictions. There was not a cloud in the vividly blue sky and it was already so hot!

My main problem this morning, however, was that of timing – notably when and what to eat. The race was due to begin at 12.30pm and we were to leave the Village more than an hour beforehand to ensure that we would not be held up in the traffic heading for the stadium. Moreover, I wanted to eat at least two hours before the start. My meal would have to be breakfast and lunch combined and I would have to finish it before half-past ten. I decided on my usual pre-race snack – scrambled egg on toast – early enough and light enough to avoid stomach trouble in the early stages of the race, yet sufficient in quantity to last me to the finish without my suffering the dreaded 'knock', so named from the suddenness with which hunger pains could strike in the last six miles, leaving one as weak as a kitten. (It is fashionable now to refer to this phenomenon as 'hitting the wall'.)

'Why not eat something during the race then?' you well might ask. After all, we had been asked for our individual requirements, which would be provided for at the 'feeding stations' or 'watering points' every five miles or so. I always trained myself to abstain from taking solids or even liquids during races after one unfortunate experience in the later stages of the 1953 AAA Marathon Championship at Cardiff when, after drinking a mixture of glucose and water, I simply lost interest in that race, my sole concern being to get to the final watering point for my next little bottle. I was astonished, however, to note that on today's list one Canadian competitor was asking for half an apple at ten miles. I could think of nothing more calculated to tie one in knots!

My own requirements were simple. As I didn't want to break stride at the feeding stations, I asked for a wet cloth to be thrown to my left hand and a pail of water to be held up to my right. I always carried a little sponge strapped by elastic to my right hand, which I intended to dip into the pail as I ran past. The wet cloth in my left I would splash over my head at once, but, as in those days we could not take water on board at any intermediate points, the precious liquid on the sponge (for mopping my face) would have to last me for the next five miles.

My early 'brunch' would leave me little time for changing afterwards, so I dressed in my racing strip at once and then, noting that I would be just in time for Mass, I decided to jog down to the little hutted chapel that served as the Catholic Chaplaincy in the Village. To my surprise, the priest beckoned me on to the altar and, there and then, I served Mass dressed as I was in my blue tracksuit with 'Scotland' emblazoned across the back.

Afterwards, I had time for only the briefest of chats with Father W. McMahon, CSSR, the Games chaplain, before dashing off for my meal. On the following day, however, he presented me with a little leather-covered book entitled *My Way of Life*, a pocket edition of *St Thomas's Summa for Everyone* by Walter Farrell and Martin Healy. He had inscribed it as follows: 'A Remembrance, Joe, of your gallant race – in my estimation even greater than the "Miracle Mile", August 7 1954, B.E.G. Long to be remembered! The same morning, too, you served my Mass.' He told me that he had chosen it because of the aptness of the opening sentences of Chapter 1 ('The One God'): 'The road that stretches before the feet of a man is a challenge to his heart long before it tests the strength of his legs. Our destiny is to run to the edge of the world and beyond, off into the darkness: sure for all our blindness, secure for all our helplessness, gaily in love for all the pressure on our hearts.' It is, indeed, a precious 'remembrance', which I have treasured ever since.

The pre-race tension, so familiar to me from previous races, was now beginning even as I entered the dining hall, and I had to force myself to take enough to eat. It intensified with my dread of delays as our car threaded its way through the heavy traffic towards the stadium. It always took the same form with me – a feeling of absolute limpness in every limb, the certainty that I would never be able to last even one mile, let alone a marathon! Of course, I knew from past experience that this was one of the symptoms of the adrenalin already surging through my body and that, as soon as the gun banged, all traces of lassitude would vanish in an explosive burst of speed – sometimes, indeed, far too fast a speed. I had discovered this to my cost more than once in the past, notably in March of this year in the International Cross-Country Championships at Birmingham when I disastrously found myself among the leaders in the first mile as we left the racecourse. I resolved that today I would try to restrain myself on the opening lap of the track.

Peeling off my tracksuit in the dressing room, I proceeded to check my kit, resolutely ignoring the more extreme of Willie Carmichael's well-meant suggestions for combating the glare of the sun – no dark glasses for me and definitely no mascara smeared on my cheek bones below the eyes, but I reluctantly compromised by putting on the very long-peaked grey-blue baseball cap that we had purchased the previous afternoon. When one is tiring, the slightest difference to one's normal kit can be a source of intense irritation and I had even been known to tear off my flapping number in the course of a race. Today, however, my number, 697, was securely attached front and back. As events turned out, I was surprisingly able to thole the cap for the first ten miles before tossing it aside, but, canny Scot as I am, I had carefully inked 'Joe McGhee, Scotland' on the inside and, much to my astonishment, the sweat-stained cap was returned to me after the race! I also knotted a large white handkerchief round my neck as an additional precaution. This I did manage to wear to the finish.

Then, as the announcement came for the runners to assemble on the track, came the shock: I couldn't find my precious little hand-sponge! I must have dropped it as I entered the stadium. My stomach lurched. I just had time to wrap a handkerchief round my hand – a poor substitute but better than nothing – before emerging from the dressing room into the cauldron outside.

It was almost 12.30pm – the hottest part (86°F/30°C) of the hottest day – so baking hot, indeed, that we found the sweat dripping from us before we made a move. We jogged impatiently on the spot as we were lined up across the track. The start, however, was delayed by a bizarre incident unparalleled in the history of the marathon. There was almost a false start!

The starter raised his pistol, we tensed, half-crouching, the commands, 'On your marks! Se…t!' rang out and then, just before the shot, an official ran across the track shouting, 'Stop! Stop!' He halted in front of the man on my left and demanded, 'Where's your number? Don't you know you must wear your number front and back?' The dark-haired man, who was dressed in a normal running strip – white singlet and black shorts – and who even had a handkerchief wrapped round his wrist like some of the other competitors, muttered something unintelligible in broken English. The official repeated his demands and finally in exasperation he asked, 'Which country are you representing?'

There was a moment's silence as this unknown runner fished in the pockets of his pants and produced a card on which was inscribed the one word: 'Yugoslavia'. We realised at once that this was a crank, a crackpot trying to gatecrash the race. The man was hustled off but, just as we were settling down again to start, he returned accompanied by one of the senior officials who had left his seat in the stand to ask why this runner was not being allowed to compete. Those officials must have had very little sense of humour for, there and then, they patiently began to explain to the man that this was a closed race and that he could not compete as Yugoslavia was not part of the British Empire or Commonwealth. He was protesting in turn to the effect that he just wanted to 'run for fun'.

The competitors were by this time extremely restless; we were very keyed-up and one Australian runner gave vent to all our feelings by characteristically mouthing some very uncomplimentary things to the starter. Fearing that the crank might dash into our midst as soon as the gun went off, however, we now virtually went on strike, refusing to move until he was removed far away into the centre of the arena. I stole a hasty glance back just before we were finally sent on our way, and, to my astonishment, he was turning somersaults, alternately tearing at the grass and then his hair while the tears were streaming down his cheeks. One of the other runners was to remark to me afterwards that he wished they had stopped the rest of us madmen before we started and not let us go through with it!

Then the pistol cracked and we were off at last!

Chapter 3

The British Empire and Commonwealth Marathon Race

LITTLE MACKAY of Australia, pint-sized but confident, immediately shot into the lead. I at once jumped into second position right on his heels with Stan Cox of England at my elbow, and in this order we circled the track and emerged from the stadium to face a very steep climb up the ramp to the road above the grandstand.

My tactics were simple. Before leaving Scotland, I had been well warned by my dad and Allan Scally, my coach, to run at my own speed and on no account to try to maintain the crazy pace that the leaders – especially Jim Peters – might set in aiming at a new world record. Though I made them the promise, I still had that little spark of ambition, however, feeling that my full capabilities had never yet been reached, so I privately determined to shadow the leaders until the moment came when I judged that I could not finish the race if I tried to maintain their pace. I would then let them go and concentrate on finishing. I had no illusions about even being placed, far less winning. I was competing, after all, against the fastest marathon runners in the world, and, despite my own Scottish record, I was not reckoned among the top competitors in this race. Even to finish among the first six would have been a tremendous achievement for me.

You can imagine my feelings, then, when approaching the road above the stadium, Mackay suddenly dropped back and, to my horror, I found myself in front, leading under conditions in which I would consider myself lucky if I did finish. I at once slackened off and the pace slowed almost to a crawl. It must have seemed almost pantomimic to the spectators lining the route to witness this 'after you – no, after you' attitude as we ambled along uphill along the tramlines.

This cautious cat-and-mouse game did not last for long, however. About quarter of a mile from the stadium, Stan Cox lost patience and spurted ahead. He was not in the least overawed by Jim Peters's reputation, believing that under such extreme weather conditions and on so tough and hilly a course, he had a good chance of winning, and, this early in the race, he was showing us that he really meant business. I at once accelerated and fell into step at his elbow.

It wasn't long before I could tell by the grunting behind me that Jim Peters had moved close up. Sneaking a sideways glance back, I saw him right on my heels accompanied by the two Australians, Kevin Mackay and Allan Lawrence. We five seemed to have broken from the field already.

Jim had a most deceptively ugly-looking style, his head jerking forward and his arms swinging so awkwardly and, at times, so violently across his body that he had been known even to cut his chest with his thrusting thumbnail. To the uninformed spectators, he might appear to be suffering badly even in the early stages of a race, but we, his fellow competitors, were not deceived.

The crowds lining the closed-off route round the city were most encouraging to us, but at times I seemed to be singled out for special applause – so much so that Peters muttered a comment about the number of friends I had. I didn't waste breath replying that it was the same Falkirk family (the Jackie Liddells), who, by a judicious use of side roads, kept reappearing at junctions over these opening miles.

I was surprised when the confident Mackay dropped back so early at three miles and then Lawrence at four miles. The Australians were obviously respecting the conditions. When five miles were passed in a modest time of over 27 minutes, Peters remarked that it was two minutes too slow. (It was certainly fast enough for me!) Yet he still held back. I was running quite comfortably and, indeed, at seven miles a press photograph shows me even slightly ahead of the two Englishmen.

Peters had given me some idea of his plans, however. (Clearly, he did not consider me a real threat!) I was not surprised, therefore, when, between eight and nine miles, he chose his psychological moment as we were about to tackle one of the notorious long hills on the course and suddenly launched himself into a tremendous spurt. Cox, he had told me, was strong on the hills, so he had decided to attack his friend and rival before Cox could make his own move. In these conditions, the pace was clearly suicidal for me and, resisting the challenge, I at once dropped back. Cox, however, plainly not in the least overawed by Peters's reputation, still tried to hang on, determination writ large in every thrusting stride, but the race soon developed into a procession – Peters a white speck in the distance with Cox vainly labouring to prevent the gap widening. The heat was now becoming so unbearable that I couldn't even endure the irritation of my long-peaked baseball cap and finally cast it aside at ten miles.

For the next eight miles I ran completely alone with only the white vest of Cox in the far distance to aim at –

Peters had soon disappeared completely from view – and I grew more and more uncomfortable as the heat began to take its toll. Then the clapping and cheers of the crowd warned me of the approach of another runner. Just before 18 miles, Allan Lawrence, the Australian, passed me smoothly and confidently and the gap opened astonishingly quickly. I just couldn't do a thing about it!

This was the beginning of my personal crisis. Certainly, I felt bad but the trouble was more psychological than physical: I simply could not visualise myself completing the eight miles still ahead. I plodded on and, then, at 19 miles, I saw a most cheering sight – Lawrence sitting disconsolately by the kerb! His encouraging remark, 'Go on, Jock,' spurred me on for only a short distance, however, and, though I was now back in bronze medal position again, I still could not see myself finishing.

Indeed, I ran past the 20-mile mark grimacing horribly at Willie Carmichael. Remembering my promise to my dad and Allan, I was determined not to drop out, but I was hoping desperately that Willie would be merciful and pull me out. His response was simply to scowl at me and gruffly urge me on. I swerved, half-twisted to glare back at him, stumbled and found myself running into a high jaggy hedge. The prickles and my resentment at Willie stung me into an all-too-short-lived burst of speed.

A mile or so later, however, I was heartened once more (but again too briefly!) by the news that Stan Cox was being taken away in an ambulance. Someone remarked that he had collapsed into a lamp-post. Incredibly, I was now in second place with less than five miles to go. It might just as well have been 50! My spasm of elation had evaporated and the black pall of depression settled down once again as I endured the next mile, stumbling more than once as I misjudged my step at street intersections.

Then, at a road junction between 22 and 23 miles, I began to hear that ominous rhythmic clapping behind me again: someone was obviously catching me up. Crossing a junction, I tripped on a kerb – or was it the tramlines? I didn't waste time in finding out for the shock of the stumble jolted me into full awareness of the situation. I glanced back to see the two South Africans, Jackie Mekler and Johan Barnard, barely 30 to 40 yards behind. Subconsciously I had been expecting them. Accustomed to ultra-long distances and to even hotter conditions, and with the reputation of being slow canny starters, they had been reckoned the obvious threat in the closing stages if conditions had been tough – and they couldn't have been tougher!

It was at that very moment, however, that my personal miracle occurred, demonstrating conclusively the power of the mind over the body. I suddenly realised that I was going to finish those last three miles and, with that realisation, my energies and my racing instincts came surging back! Turning the next corner (to my right), I plunged into the crowd of spectators at the edge of the pavement. The loudspeaker van kept blaring, 'Come into the middle of the road, Joe. It's much clearer here.' But, hidden by the spectators, I was not offering myself as a target to the following pair. I knew that, at the top of this hill, the route turned left for a short distance (perhaps 50 yards) before abruptly swinging right again, and I gathered my energies. Bursting from the crowd, I spurted flat-out to reach the farther corner before my pursuers rounded the first. Then I settled down into a more comfortable racing pace.

I did not dare risk a glance back over the next 2½ miles in case I should offer the slightest encouragement to the chasing South Africans. I was determined now to fight every inch for that silver medal. The thought of gold never entered my head even when, near the stadium, spectators began shouting that the man in front was looking bad. Jim Peters's deceptively awkward style, however, always gave that impression of painful effort. My main concern was how I was going to tackle the last steep hill (1 in 10 gradient) that led up past the stadium to almost the roof level of the grandstand.

I had just reached the foot and was gathering myself for the effort when the news of Peters's collapse was yelled to me. My first reaction was one of complete panic. How close were the South Africans behind? I risked a glance back. As far as the eye could see – a good 300 yards or more – there was no runner in sight! I knew then that I could not be beaten and I have never felt better in any race. The hill held no terrors for me now as I faced the climb if not exactly with zest, then certainly with determination.

As I turned right to run down the steep ramp past the stands into the stadium, I was struck by the deathly hush. The crowd had been shocked into silence by Peters's collapse. 'What is the next man going to be like?' seemed to be the question uppermost in everyone's mind. They did not even know who was coming next, so little news of the marathon had percolated back to the stadium. There, below me, framed in the opening on to the track, stood the tall track-suited figure of Dr Euan Douglas, the Scottish team captain. I have never seen such a look of utter stupefaction on anyone's face as realisation dawned and then the big hammer thrower, dolphin-like, began to leap up and down waving his arms.

I ran into sheer pandemonium. I have never received such a reception. The crowd's reaction, one of the Scottish swimmers later informed me, must have been one of immense relief that this runner was not in a state of collapse. My ears were literally popping with the din as I raced round the track towards the tape to become, at 25, the youngest marathon winner in the history of the Games.

I prize in particular one print of a press photograph taken just after I had finished. It shows the three of us – myself, Willie Carmichael and Euan Douglas – walking round the grass inside the track towards the dressing rooms. It has, of course, its value as a testimony to how fit I was looking. Indeed, if it hadn't been for the dirt on my right knee and the sweat stain on my singlet, it could even have been taken for a photograph prior to the start! The situation, however, seems odd – not a smile on any of our faces! Willie, in the middle of the group, seems to be sternly haranguing me. On the outside, next to the track, with set jaw, my face turned away from him, I am eyeing warily something on the stand-side of the track ahead of me. Euan is turning away from the two us, inwards to the centre of the arena. 'What on earth is the fight about?' I have been often asked. Usually, I reply jokingly that I'm being told that I am not being allowed to attend the closing ball that night. In reality, Willie is advising me to hurry straight into the showers without stopping to say anything to the horde of reporters clustered round the exit below the stand.

It was only as the call came for the victory ceremony for the marathon, however, that the realisation of the enormity and sheer unexpectedness of my achievement began to sink in. Excitement had banished all trace of weariness as I emerged once more out into the sun-soaked arena. I remember stopping briefly to congratulate Roger Bannister as he was coming in from the mile victory ceremony. Though I had chatted in the Games Village with John Landy, a most approachable and unassuming world record holder, this was the first time that I had met the legendary Bannister.

As we climbed on to the podium, Jackie Mekler, the South African silver medallist, and I exchanged friendly congratulations. The third man, Johan Barnard, however, was being carried barefooted to the ceremony on a stretcher. I have a beautiful picture of my leaning down sideways to support him with my outstretched left arm as he was being held erect by a senior Scout and an ambulance man. The two of us are smiling broadly, however. Physically, he seemed not too bad except for his feet. It seems that his shoes had had to be cut off!

The victory ceremony as the Scottish saltire was raised will remain an unforgettable memory for me. We turned to our right to face the huge scoreboard, topped appropriately with the picture of a girl in full Highland dress, and displaying the legend:

1.
Scotland

2.
South Africa

3.
South Africa

as a full band played (in the correct tempo this time!) 'Scots Wha Hae'. It was, indeed, a fairytale ending for the small Scottish team too, for us to win our first athletics gold medal just as the Games were drawing to a close.

Chapter 4

Why Did Jim Peters Fail?

IN THIS account, I have been attempting to answer the question of *what* actually did happen in this historic race. I have only indirectly touched upon the question of *why* such a disaster occurred to Peters at all – and to Cox too, for that matter, for England should comfortably have won both gold and silver medals.

It is not enough to point to the extremely hot weather conditions and the hilly nature of the course – or even the possibility that the course might have been too long, as Jim, despite the assurances of the Games' officials to the contrary, averred. After all, these conditions were the same for everyone, and, when you race in the marathon, you are competing not only against the other runners but the elements and the nature of the terrain as well, and you have to adapt accordingly. In recording 2hrs 39mins 36secs, I personally ran over half a minute more slowly per mile than I was capable of. Peters obviously did not. A world record time was simply out of the question that day. The whole point of the exercise, surely, was to win the medal and each of us was chosen by our respective countries to do just that. I managed to do so. Jim did not. A 'glorious failure' is all very well but it does not disguise the fact that he ran an unintelligent race. As Sir Arthur Porritt, general chairman of the Games, succinctly summed up: 'He ran his race and failed.'

Nevertheless, the question still remains: why did the best and most experienced marathon runner in the world run – or was allowed to run – himself into such a state?

One main reason, obviously, was that Jim wished to record a very fast time – in fact, a new world record. He had been lowering the figure in almost all his recent races and this championship was the perfect showcase for another record. He was, indeed, a perfectionist – hence his pre-race worries that the conditions might detract from the winning time. Besides, big-hearted as he was, he knew no other way to compete except by giving his all in every race and he would run flat-out, leaving the opposition trailing far in his wake. I know of no other runner who could punish himself like Jim. Indeed, Neil Allen in the *London Evening Standard* (19 April 1996) quoted Jim's own words: 'When the gun sounds, you go out there to kill or be killed.' Commenting, too, on Jim's approach at aiming for the fastest possible time and his ability to push himself to the very limits, Percy Cerutty, the famous Australian coach, declared that it meant his races could either be record-breaking wins – or 'glorious failures' (as in Vancouver and the earlier Helsinki Olympics!). Even in training, Jim's attitude was exactly the same. 'Jogging or shuffling had no part in my make-up,' he explained in a letter to the *Scots Athlete* (November 1954). 'There never was time to muck about. The maximum hard work had to be done in the shortest possible time.'

There was, however, another factor – probably the most influential of all. Jim reckoned that Stan Cox was his greatest rival in this race and that, under these conditions, Stan had a real chance of beating him on the day. He could safely express such apprehensions to me and, indeed, give me some idea of his probable tactics, as I was such a rank outsider. I remember, in particular, the Monday morning of our second week in Vancouver when the two of us ran behind Cox from mile 11 to mile 19 of the course – I with my ankle all strapped up.

Stan, for his part, gave me the impression that he clearly thought well of his own ability to defeat Jim in this championship. He knew that one of his greatest assets was his strength in tackling the hills – and this course certainly had plenty of them! He would, of course, also have in mind the fact that Jim had endured a strength-sapping race in taking a well-deserved bronze medal in the Six Miles Championship the previous Saturday.

Thus we had the paradoxical situation that the two English team-mates were, in reality, rivals and, as I have already described, Jim adapted his tactics to kill off the opposition – notably Stan. If, on the other hand, they had really run together as a team, at a sensible speed, supporting and pacing each other – at least until the closing stages of the race, England would easily have collected the first two medals, the disaster would have been averted and, instead of being such a 'cause célèbre' over so many years, the 1954 Vancouver Marathon would long ago have been forgotten.

The final summing-up of the race I leave to Jim himself. He was magnanimous in acclaiming me publicly in that 1996 *Evening Standard* article referred to above: 'Joe is the man who deserves every credit for having won on that terrible day. He was and remains the winner.'

P.S. I did not arrive back in Scotland until the Saturday following the race, so missed the press furore during that first week. Apparently, most of the publicity had concentrated on lauding Jim's 'glorious failure' and thus had provoked a furious backlash, at least in Scotland, from irate readers. By the time of my return, most of the Scottish newspapers had changed their attitude. This situation was described to me by my friend and mentor, Joe Walker, who was stung into drafting a letter to the *Daily Express*, which he delayed sending until he had obtained my approval. He sent it to me on the 12th. As his draft also contains one of the best assessments of the race and my own part in it, I append copies of both his letters:

12-8-54

Dear Joe,
I am enclosing a letter which I wrote last Tuesday and intended to send to The Daily Express after I had shown it to you for your approval.

With your delayed return and the sudden change in the publicity given to you by The Daily Express during the last few days I think the time and opportunity has now passed for sending the letter. I note from Friday's issue of the paper that they have received many letters on the same subject and therefore I am sure they would not print it.

However it will express what I am sure all athletes in Scotland are thinking about The Daily Express.

Hope you are feeling fine and looking forward to seeing you soon.

With best wishes
J. F. Walker

* * *

Scottish Daily Express,
Albion Street,
Glasgow, C1.

Dear Sir,
British Empire Games, 1954 Marathon Race
I note from Wednesday's issue of The Scottish Daily Express that you are proposing to strike a medal to be awarded to Jim Peters in commemoration of his 'historic performance' in the marathon race at Vancouver in the British Empire Games, 1954.

Ever since the result of the race was published in The Scottish Daily Express on Monday I have been shocked at your press treatment of the event. Your write-up of the event savours very much of the man bites dog story.

The conditions of the race were the same for all the competitors, hilly course, very hot conditions, start at noon, watering points etc. Probably the English competitors would have the best of coaches, masseurs etc. in attendance. The English competitors, Peters and Cox, were the most experienced in the race and in ability many minutes faster than the next best in the race. Yet in spite of all their advantages one of them ran into a telegraph pole and rendered himself unconscious, the other built up a lead of almost 19 minutes over McGhee in conditions which are reported to have been intolerably hot, thus rendering himself a pitiful sight when he entered the arena. A gross error of judgement according to press reports would appear to have been made by such an experienced runner as

Peters in running himself into such a state, by his attendants in allowing him in such intolerable conditions to build up such a lead of 19 minutes that he had not sufficient energy to finish the course and lastly by the lack of medical advisers to withdraw him from the race long before he came near the arena.

I write as President of St Modan's Amateur Athletic Club to protest strongly at the lack of publicity given by a Scottish paper to the magnificent effort of a young Scottish athlete who actually won the race.

McGhee was Scotland's sole representative in the race and therefore had not the advantage of many of the competitors who had team-mates with them. In comparison to the experienced Peters he was very immature and yet he was able to overcome all the physical and natural difficulties which Peters experienced and according to the press reports McGhee finished strongly. His victory was the culminating point of many months of strenuous individual effort and the carrying out of the instructions of his well-wishers which he received before he left Scotland. His instructions were very simple: 'Run your race, let Peters and Cox go on themselves.' 'Remember to keep a bit in hand for the finish as marathon races are won in the last few miles.'

Very little has been written about the story behind McGhee's magnificent effort in winning the race. His membership since his schooldays of St Modan's AAC, one of the smallest athletic clubs in Scotland with a mere handful of active athletes and which celebrates its coming of age this year. The marathon section of the club never at any time consisted of more than two or three enthusiasts. His training in the morning, at lunchtime, in the evening, at the weekends and running from his RAF station to his home all in an effort to cover approximately 100 miles per week. This season he has run approximately over 3,000 miles and with the exception of races most of that distance was run alone. Within the last year in order to gain competitive experience he joined in addition Shettleston Harriers. He has competed in probably less than six major marathon races in his life yet he was able to beat the pick of 24 countries from the British Empire.

Let us not forget the glorious effort of the winner in glorifying what appears from press reports to have been a gross error of judgement on behalf of the English competitors and their officials.

Personally I don't think Peters will be grateful for any medal commemorating such a performance and I would respectfully suggest that the efforts of The Scottish Daily Express would be more suitably directed to commemorating the historic performance of the Scottish team at the Games.

Yours faithfully
J. F. Walker
President, St Modan's AAC

(See Chapter 11 – 'Five Inspirers' for my own tribute to Joe Walker.)

Chapter 5

Welcome Home

THERE ARE some events at which I was not present but that, by hearing the vivid and repeated accounts over the years, I can visualise far more clearly than many others I actually experienced. Such an event was the hearing of my victory by my family back home. Because of the time difference, the first reference to the marathon was on the radio news at ten o'clock that night. At that stage, the race was still in progress and I was mentioned in third place. Everyone was over the moon. I had prepared them too well about how poor my chances were! My dad said that they were praying desperately that I could only hold that position. They were all on tenterhooks until the next bulletin at midnight when the announcer began by simply giving the names of the first three finishers. At the words, 'First, J. McGhee, Scotland,' complete bedlam broke out as neighbours poured out of their houses and came running from all directions to our home. My dad always remarked at this point in his story that he had never seen so many nightdresses in his life!

For me in Vancouver, however, it was all rather an anticlimax and, indeed, the following week remains a bit of a blur to me. I did go to the closing ball that Saturday night and had to be up extremely early the following morning to fit in Mass before catching the train to the USA.

The proposal had been made to me that I should fly back with the first home-going contingent of British competitors, but I had resisted on the grounds that I was competing in the last event of the Games and wanted some free time to relax afterwards. Finally, I succeeded in being allocated to the last returning plane on the following Tuesday. After all, I wanted to make use of my American visa!

In those days, it was extremely difficult to obtain a visa to enter the States, but, before leaving for Canada, I had phoned the American consulate in Edinburgh and, posing as the adjutant at RAF Turnhouse, said that one of our officers would be arriving that afternoon for a visa. I got the visa all right but only after having every one of my fingers (both hands!) printed.

Only five others of the entire Scottish party had managed to obtained visas – diver Peter Heatly and Bertha, his wife, the swimmers Elinor Gordon and Margaret Girvan, and Willie Carmichael himself. The six of us, advised and given introductions by a Vancouver businessman, Sam Mackay, were determined to visit Seattle, the nearest American big city.

That Sunday was one of the oddest I have ever spent. We visited two very affluent, modern homes and the only food that we were offered during that entire day was cocktail sticks with our drinks! The four swimmers in our party swam in the open-air pool in the garden. I remember, however, becoming more and more sleepy – the only reaction I was feeling to my efforts of the day before – and I decided to have a shower to try to revive myself. Peter and I could hear the girls through the wall and their complaint was the same as ours. We were starving! It was not until late that evening after saying goodbye to our hosts that we managed to find a restaurant where the six of us ordered the thickest and most enormous T-bone steaks I have ever seen. We certainly did justice to them!

One amusing incident I do remember from that day concerned Willie. He was extremely proud of our little group and boasted that all four of the competitors with him were Empire and Commonwealth gold medallists. Peter Heatly still recalls one of our American hostesses then innocently asking, 'How did our boys [i.e. Americans] do?' and his reply that they had forfeited their chance to compete 200 years before!

We had only time and money for one night in a hotel, where I shared a room with Willie, and then a brief visit to the downtown shops, where I bought myself some nylon drip-dry shirts, not yet seen in Scotland, before we had to head back to Vancouver. Money was quite a problem for us as our government at this time would allow travellers to take only £44 out of the country. Luckily, I had taken the limit and, of course, I had not needed to spend much in the three weeks up till then.

The journey home was a nightmare, taking days longer than the outward one! A stopover in Montreal, however, was the brightest spot. Seeing the city this time in daylight, I was struck by how much more at home I felt. The buildings were older and more European in appearance in contrast to those in Vancouver, which seemed so much more American and unfamiliar to us then. The last half-century in this country, of course, has seen such an Americanisation in our lifestyle, architecture, shopping habits, TV programmes and films that such contrasts in atmosphere have largely disappeared. When Elinor Gordon decided to make a brief visit to a relative, Margaret Girvan and I accompanied her in the taxi. We then went on to see

Mount Royal, the world's most famous shrine to St Joseph. The three churches built one on top of the other were a most impressive sight.

Leaving Montreal, we then experienced a seemingly interminable wait at Gander, which was extremely boring and depressing. We had to endure the bleak outlook from the airport for many hours while engine repairs were carried out on our aircraft. Eventually, it was early on the Saturday morning before we finally touched down at Prestwick, nearly two days later than we had expected!

I was completely unprepared for the welcome I received at Prestwick and then much more so at Falkirk. The press had ignored me on our departure for Vancouver, but now, last off the plane, I found myself besieged by photographers. I have some wonderful pictures of my dad, mum and my sister, Louise, in the airport lounge. They had been brought to Prestwick by one of the daily newspapers.

Eventually we headed off home to Falkirk where I was overwhelmed by my reception. Turning into Windsor Road, I was astonished to see the street lined with flags and bunting and, 300 yards along, our house and garden decorated with huge Scottish flags. An archway with the town coat of arms and a banner, 'Well Done Joe', surmounted the steps leading up to our garden (which was raised five feet above the road). I had been persuaded to stand up through the opening roof of the car as we drove slowly along, horn hooting, and, before we could stop at our house, we were surrounded by people pouring from their homes to augment the cheering crowd already blocking the road outside.

Apparently, events had been building up all week. The national news media had at first so concentrated on the Peters tragedy that little mention had been made of me, with the possible exception of Dunky Wright's full back-page spread in the *Sunday Express* – 'I Know How Joe McGhee Feels'. Then the indignation of the Scottish public – especially the Falkirk Bairns – set up a corresponding reaction. Some of the hurried and imaginative attempts to redress the balance were laughable. One of the tabloids, for example, at the end of that year featured Peter Wilson's article in which he attempted to make up for his complete omission of my name when he had concentrated on describing Peters' suffering at the time. He only made matters worse! Under the headline 'Ginger For Pluck McGhee' (I was dark-haired!), he went on to refer to the 'diminutive Falkirk runner'! Poor communications too and the delays at Gander airport had resulted in conflicting reports about when I would be arriving home and had caused hurried revisals in the welter of preparations that seemed to have involved everyone from the Provost to the local bands.

We were besieged by well-wishers and I was virtually a prisoner in the house for most of that day. We had to bring in a barber, Johnny McKenna, a friend and neighbour, to cut my hair, and, to get rid of the press, I even had to suffer the indignity of being photographed in the bath, insisting, however, that the light was held by my Uncle Charlie and not the young lady reporter who was accompanying the photographer! In the following weeks and later years, however, I learned how to put off photographers who wanted to devise unusual and invariably stupid situations for me, by saying that other newspapers had already taken such a picture. The ploy always worked!

That Saturday evening we were all taken to the Regal Cinema and we sat in the front row of the balcony with Provost Watson to see the Pathé newsreel of the Vancouver Games. It showed the start of the marathon, Bannister's mile victory, Peters' collapse and my finish in the stadium.

One press photograph of our group showed the concern on all our faces as the full horror of Jim's state became apparent. I had not realised just how agonising and prolonged it had been. Then, as my towel-clad smiling face appeared on the screen with the announcer's closing remarks, the cinema erupted into loud cheers. I had then to appear on the stage before the screen to receive from the manager of the cinema the actual news film that had just been screened. I still have this copy, which, of course, has never again been used as it would require a large cinema-sized projector to run it. The manager, however, promised to obtain for me a 16mm copy, which arrived very promptly. This copy was later overused to accompany the many talks that I was invited to give by a wide variety of organisations. Some of them, indeed, (without my permission!) quite unscrupulously cut the earlier items of news on the film and rather amateurishly respliced them again.

Chapter 6

A Hectic Three Months

(Presentations, Social Events and Races)

THUS BEGAN the increasingly hectic next three months – an intricate balancing act into which I had to fit the demands of work, resuming my training and coping with a growing and at times irrelevant round of social functions.

Apart from going to church the next morning, I stayed indoors all day, though even here I was not immune from a stream of visits from friends and neighbours – and more reporters. Luckily, at this time, we were not yet on the telephone! On the Monday, the 16th, however, my leave up, I had to return to my RAF duties to be greeted with the congratulations of my colleagues and the news that the promotion board examination results had come through after I had left for Canada and that I was no longer flying officer but flight lieutenant. The CO's first question was, 'How are you feeling?' Fortunately, my first words in reply were, 'Tired, sir!' He then at once gave me extra leave, which I took from the beginning of September till the 14th. Later that morning I had my first run since the marathon and astonished myself by recording one of my fastest times for the ten-mile Turnhouse course.

The social whirl then began in earnest and I did not manage another run till the Thursday, when I ran an even faster ten miles, and then a fast 5½ miles on the Saturday morning to log only 25½ miles for this first week back. I remember noting, however, that I was running well and not suffering any effects from my efforts in the marathon. My first social event had been on the Tuesday of that first week back when I had to attend a formal lunch in the mess with Air Marshall Sir Charles Guest, the Inspector General of the RAF. The CO embarrassed me by announcing to everyone that the guest of honour was myself and not the Inspector General!

That evening I had then to travel to Glasgow for a BBC radio recording. I was the guest on the *Jimmy Logan Show* and had to join in some humorous patter with Jimmy about his friend and rival, Stanley Baxter. As soon as I saw the large studio audience, however, I almost caused consternation by not holding up my script and ad-libbing my replies, looking directly towards the audience. Jimmy at once stuck his copy of the script up in front of me! Some of the jokes, I must admit, were rather 'corny': for example, Jimmy, seeking advice on getting fit, said, 'I'm bothered with my breathing,' to which my reply was, 'I'll soon put a stop to that!' My 'spot' on the show (and my one and only experience of 'show business') ended with a duet in which I had to sing with Jimmy alternate lines of an instantly forgettable ditty to the tune of 'If You Ever Go Across the Sea to Ireland'.

Next day, Wednesday, I was invited to lunch in Edinburgh with the RAF Turnhouse chaplain, Canon McClelland, and in the evening I was guest at the Falkirk FC versus Hearts match. I have an excellent photograph of my shaking hands with the teams on the pitch before kick-off. On the Friday I had lunch again with the chaplain and my colleagues at Turnhouse and on Saturday I was a guest at a very wet Edinburgh Highland Games at Murrayfield, followed in the evening by dinner in the City Chambers and a visit to the Edinburgh Tattoo. So ended my first week home – a very busy one, indeed!

The second week was even more hectic and, looking back, I am surprised how I managed to fit in a total of 40¼ miles training and my RAF duties. On the Sunday evening I gave a talk to officers on a course at Carronvale, the Boys' Brigade Headquarters, where I was presented with a copy of the life of their founder. Then on Wednesday, 25th, I spoke and gave a film presentation of the race in Stirling to my old school, St Modan's High, where I had been both pupil and teacher prior to entering the RAF. The following afternoon I visited St Mungo's High School in Falkirk, where my former principal teacher in the English department at St Modan's, Paddy Gallagher, was now rector. The next evening I was a guest at the retiral presentation in Falkirk to my former headmaster at St Francis Primary School, Mr John Farrell, a family friend as well.

The highlight of this week, however, was my arrival at Cowal Highland Gathering on Saturday, 28th. Dunky Wright and I flew, by helicopter, from Glasgow airport to Dunoon where we touched down in the middle of the rainy Games arena and I did a quarter of a mile lap of honour.

Thankfully, the next week was less hectic. I began my fortnight's leave on Wednesday, 1 September and was able to manage 89 miles training over six days for the week, recording my fastest times so far for my Slamannan 12-mile circuit on the Wednesday and the Falkirk-Castlecary-Dunipace 20.2-mile course on the Friday.

Nevertheless, I was unable to fit in any run at all on Thursday, 2nd. I had lunch with my mentor, Joe Walker, at the Glasgow Royal Technical College (now Strathclyde University), and, afterwards, I was the only 'live' guest of Howard M. Lockhart on his BBC radio programme, *Personal Choice*. He managed to talk me out of my initial choice of record, Harry Lauder's 'Keep Right On to the End of the Road' – the marathon runner's theme song I called it! – and persuade me to substitute the much more romantic song, 'Come to Me, Bend to Me' from the musical *Brigadoon* as this choice enabled me to tell the story of the Scottish girls' embarrassment (which I mentioned earlier) during our visit to the open-air theatre that evening in Vancouver.

The following week, my second week's leave, saw a return to relative normality for me and I was able to concentrate on my training again. I managed to log a total of 92½ miles in seven runs over six days, beginning with a slowish 20 miles on the Sunday and ending with another faster 20 miles on the Saturday. My blank day, the Friday, was spent in Glasgow with Charlie, my brother, home on leave from the RAF. We were trying unsuccessfully to get ideas for the presentations planned by both the Windsor Road area committee and Falkirk Town Council.

It seems incredible now when so many training grants, expenses, appearance money, etc. are lavished on our full-time 'amateur' athletes that in 1954 the governing bodies of our sport were so exceedingly pernickety in enforcing their extremely parsimonious rules regarding money limits. (More of this in detail later!) We were not allowed to accept presentations valued at more than £11. The Town Council told me that this was a serious problem for them as they had planned a civic reception for me to include also the local Air Training Corps team, who had won for the sixth time the Battle of Britain trophy for shooting. They therefore asked me not to choose a watch as it must, of course, be inferior to the watches already bought for the cadets. The Windsor Road Committee was similarly perplexed, having collected £40, and several weird and wonderful suggestions were made, including even the erection of memorial gates to our local strip of parkland!

By one means or another, I managed to solve both problems but they did play havoc with my attempts to get back into a more normal training routine. In fact, the next week, beginning 12 September, I was able to fit in only 39½ miles. Instead of my intended very long Sunday run, I managed only ten miles before lunch, as I had to visit Nunraw Abbey in the Borders in the afternoon. The next two days I failed to train at all as I went to Glasgow again on both days. On the Monday, I was invited to the Kelvin Hall Exhibition and, on that visit, fortuitously, I was able to fix up Falkirk Town Council's presentation gift. I was introduced to the manager of a restaurant in the Argyle Arcade who in turn introduced me to a jeweller in the Arcade. He drastically reduced the price of a four-piece silver-plated tea service and sold it for £11 to the Council who then had it suitably inscribed.

The next day, returning to Glasgow, I accompanied one of the local MPs on a visit to the Remington Rand factory at Hillington where I solved the Windsor Road presentation problem. The manager wanted to give me their latest portable typewriter as a free gift. He was astonished when I told him that I was unable to accept but business rules unfortunately would not permit him to sell the machine for the £11 that the committee was allowed. It had to be free or full price. However, he did suggest an ingenious compromise. A batch of portables that had been ordered by the Dutch army had been returned as rust had got into the consignment. He promised to pick out the best one and sell it for the stipulated £11. I collected the 'damaged' item the following week. It was, in fact, in mint condition except for a tiny spot of rust on the head of one of the tiny screws holding the rubber feet to the base! We were still faced, however, with the question of what had to be done with the remaining £29 that the committee had collected. They were delighted by my suggesting that we could get round the problem by having three presentations: the main one from the committee, another from the old folks in the area and one from the children. The remaining money I wanted them to spend on wines and sweets for the old people at their function. In all, I received from my local friends and neighbours my typewriter, a leather briefcase, a dictionary and a gold Parker pen!

Despite these jaunts to Glasgow and elsewhere, my running did not seem to be suffering. I recorded my fastest time so far for the Turnhouse 15-mile circuit on the Wednesday and won my first race since Vancouver on Saturday, 18 September, Shettleston's 3½ Miles Road Trial, finishing ahead of both Eddie Bannon and Clark Wallace, who had beaten me the year before, and, in the process, I recorded the fast time of 16mins 17secs, almost half a minute faster than my time in 1953. The following week, too, saw my mileage total rise to almost 90 miles, thanks to a 21-mile run home in the evening from Turnhouse on the Tuesday, and despite having to return to Glasgow to Remington Rand and Shettleston Swimming Gala on the Wednesday. The biggest test of my fitness, however, came at the end of the week when I had my first open competition since the Empire and Commonwealth Games, this time in Fort William.

So strong were we as a club at this time that Shettleston Harriers could afford to call ourselves 'Lanarkshire' and compete effectively against full county teams. Two memorable and lavishly hospitable trips were to sports meetings at Fort William against Lochaber this September and at Elgin against Morayshire the following summer.

At Fort William, I was slotted down to compete in a distance race against a strong field including two past winners of the Ben Nevis race, Brian Kearney and Eddie Campbell. I suggested that, as their last major races were up the Ben and mine was the 26-mile marathon, we should compromise with a seven-mile race. They agreed! The course consisted of six laps of heavy grass track and the rest flat road. It really was no contest. I set off at a tremendous pace before the crowd and won by nearly 600 yards from my clubmate, Walter McFarlane, in the fast time of 34mins 36secs. (At the Elgin meeting the following year, I again ran against Eddie Campbell to set a record time for the 24 miles from Elgin to Forres and back.)

After lunch on the Sunday before we left for the south again, Eddie Campbell took me on a 5½-mile run from the Fort William Youth Centre up Glen Nevis as far as the youth hostel and back. This was the nearest I was ever to get to the Ben itself. Eddie quashed any hopes I might have entertained of tackling the Ben race one day by advising me strongly against it if I still had marathon aspirations. I knew I could hold my own with anyone up to the summit. The dangers lay in the recklessness of the descent by many competitors. I had stimulated in Eddie, however, the ambition to run again in the Marathon Championship and, by now a firm friend of mine, he travelled south to our home in Falkirk the following summer and managed to win his standard medal in the championship.

Next day, back to my RAF duties at Turnhouse, I broke my fastest time for my 15-mile lunchtime run, and, despite having to fit in two presentations, managed to keep my training going that week to total 75½ miles. The week, indeed, ended on a high note with my toughest test since Vancouver when I ran the anchor leg for our quartet in the McAndrew Trophy Road Relay round a 3¼-mile circuit at

Victoria Park in Glasgow. This was the traditional opener to the new winter season for clubs throughout Scotland. I took over the lead on the last lap ahead of Ian Binnie of Victoria Park, the national three- and six-mile champion and record holder, and my team-mate in Vancouver. I felt very sluggish over the first 2½ miles and, knowing that he was chasing me hard, I chopped my stride and tried to force myself faster. I really hated my role as pacemaker! Inevitably, with his long flowing stride, he caught me not long after we passed Jordanhill College, but we had still over half a mile to go and he had made the mistake of passing me too early. Gathering my strength, I immediately thrust past him again and took him by surprise on the hill. Sensing a break, I began a long sprint up the straight towards the crowds round the finish and won by 12 seconds. Binnie seemed happy enough with establishing a new record but I was even more elated by my time of 15mins 28½secs, the second-fastest time of the 248 competitors (62 teams) and 49 seconds faster than my own best time in the past. The fact, too, that the third-fastest was the national mile champion (Small) and the fourth was the national cross-country champion (Bannon) was conclusive proof to me that my marathon training, far from slowing me, had actually sharpened up considerably my speed over the much shorter distances.

The two presentations this week had been memorable affairs. On the Wednesday evening, the traffic on Windsor Road was again brought to a halt by the crowds as I received my typewriter from the Windsor Road Committee on the natural platform of our elevated front garden. I was proud that four of my mentors, Joe Walker, Allan Scally, Dunky Wright and, of course, my dad were guests. They were all principal guests again on the Saturday night in Glasgow at the Scottish Marathon Club's annual social when I was presented with a plaque installing me as their first honorary life member. My most embarrassing moment that evening was when Mrs Mabel Thursby recited a poem that she had written in my honour and presented me with a framed copy!

The next week, the eighth after my Vancouver win, I finally managed back into full training, recording a total of 105 miles. Although my longest session was only 15 miles at Turnhouse on the Tuesday lunchtime, I was back to two runs per day on four of the other days, including a tough ten miles cross-country in fast bursts with Bannon on the Saturday afternoon after a fast ten-mile road run on the High Bonnybridge circuit in the morning. I had, too, my usual RAF duties at Turnhouse and two very important engagements this week.

On the Wednesday evening, 6 October, Falkirk Town Council gave me a civic reception and presented me with the silver tea service with the following inscription on the teapot:

Presented to
FL/LT JOSEPH McGHEE
by the TOWN COUNCIL
on behalf of the citizens of Falkirk
as a tangible expression
of their pride
in his splendid achievement
in winning the Marathon Race
in the
BRITISH EMPIRE and
COMMONWEALTH GAMES
held at VANCOUVER on
7 August 1954

Next day, I was invited to address Falkirk Rotary Club at their luncheon. Up till now my efforts at speech-making had been mainly confined to expressions of thanks or answers to questions at functions such as sports panels. Today, however, I was expected to give a longish talk. I had no notes and decided to speak impromptu on the topic: 'What it feels like to run a marathon'. As I got into my stride, I found myself fluently describing my experiences in the Vancouver Marathon and then, with a surge of exhilaration, I suddenly discovered that I had my listeners hanging on my every word – the first time that I had really achieved every speaker's dream of complete empathy with and power over their audience. I must have far exceeded my allotted time but it did not seem to matter. The most common comment I received from this and later audiences was 'we're feeling really exhausted – as if we had been running ourselves!'

Perhaps I had been only too successful for I found myself now launched squarely on to the speaker circuit and was sought after by secretaries of all sorts of organisations, some with little or no connections with sport. The same talk, broadly, I adapted to all these diverse audiences and I became quite skilled at anticipating their reactions, knowing just where they would laugh or gasp at my apparently off-the-cuff remarks. Finally, a few years later, after a talk to a group of insurance agents, I came at last to my senses and, calling a halt to my role as itinerant entertainer, I resolutely refused such invitations, which would still arrive even years afterwards. Indeed, more than 45 years on, I was still receiving these requests. However, unlike the speakers on today's after-dinner circuit, who can command astonishingly large fees, I never received a penny for these efforts. Clearly, I lived at the wrong time! Nevertheless, I still continued to speak to schools, youth and sports clubs and was gratified that I had been successful in encouraging future champions as we shall see.

The following week, the ninth, saw at last a return to normality for me with my work and lunchtime and evening training. I logged 108 miles in 11 sessions including a 25-miler on the Sunday. At the end of the week, however, I experienced again the absurdity of some press reporting when I competed in the Lanarkshire Ten Miles Road Relay Championship (four by 2½ miles) held in Springburn, Glasgow. I ran the second leg of the relay for Shettleston, taking over in second place 50 yards behind the Springburn Harriers runner. There were two bad hills on the course and I had to drive myself hard past him before finishing very strongly to hand over a lead of 150 yards to our next runner who kept us in front. Then Bannon ran our last lap in the fastest time of the day – 14mins 51secs – to clinch the championship for us. I was delighted to be credited with the second-fastest time of all the competitors – 14mins 57½secs. Yet the headline that appeared over one of the leading Sunday paper's report of the race was 'Joe McGhee is beaten'! Incidentally, this event also demonstrated two of my training practices at this time. The distance I raced was 2½ miles, yet I ran 3¾ miles before the start, getting a knowledge of the course and treating the race not as an objective in itself but as only part of my training build-up.

My hopes of settling down now to a regular pattern of work and training, however, were shattered during the next fortnight by the increasing flood of invitations by a variety of organisations – five functions in week 10 and seven in week 11 after Vancouver! I don't know how on earth I managed to fit in any running at all, yet, somehow, I covered 74 and 66 miles in these two weeks.

On Monday, 18 October, I was invited to a literary cocktail party in the Adam Rooms, George Street, Edinburgh, to honour Sir Michael Bruce, 11th Baronet of Stenhouse and Airth, whose autobiography of an extremely adventurous life throughout the world had just been published. I had been fortunate to meet him in Canada, where it had been mentioned to me that he was the brother of Nigel Bruce, who had played Dr Watson to Basil Rathbone's Sherlock Holmes in many films. This evening, Sir Michael welcomed me very warmly again and presented me with a copy of his book, *Tramp Royal*, with the following inscription: 'To a really great Scot In memory of Vancouver Michael Bruce Bt.'

I thoroughly enjoyed the evening, not only because I was not involved in any formal speechifying but even more because I had the pleasure of meeting two of the greatest 20th-century Scottish writers, Sir Compton Mackenzie and Eric Linklater.

The following evening I enjoyed a very different occasion in Coatbridge Town Hall as a member of the *Scottish Daily Express* Sports Forum. I was to attend several of these sports panels in towns throughout the country, such as Paisley, Motherwell, Perth, Galashiels and Oban, and I revelled in the cut and thrust of impromptu debate on questions from the audience. In the process, I got to know very well some of the panellists, such as Jock Stein, Willie Waddell and Eugene Henderson (the boxing referee). Dunky Wright himself appeared on most of them and even Jim Peters on one occasion in Perth, the very day his new optician's business was opening in Essex.

This evening's forum in Coatbridge had a particular outcome that was to give me great pleasure later. At the conclusion, Willie Waddell, the Rangers winger and later manager, and I had to hurry to a taxi outside the hall when we were mobbed by a crowd of young boys waving scraps of paper and demanding autographs. Waddell pushed me into the taxi and dived in after me. A few days later,

I received a letter from a young Coatbridge teenager, Tommy Malone, who apologised for the behaviour of his companions and explained that he had really wanted my advice about joining a running club. I replied that, duty bound, I had to tell him that his local club was Monkland Harriers but that my own mentor and friend, Allan Scally of Shettleston Harriers, also coached St Bridget's youth club only a couple of miles or so away at Baillieston. Little did I realise then that he would later be competing with me in Shettleston's first team. Thin, indeed slight, in appearance, he was to develop rapidly, was third counting man in our winning national cross-country championship teams in 1961 and 1962 and played a vital role in our Edinburgh to Glasgow Road Relay successes. His greatest achievements, however, occurred after he emigrated to South Africa, where he won the renowned Comrades' Marathon, 54¼ miles over the very hilly road from Durban to Pietermaritzburg.

Tommy was not the first young runner my achievements seem to have inspired, however. During the week after I had returned from Canada, the seven-year-old son of the neighbouring Young family caused a lot of worry when he disappeared and was found jogging along the road nearly at Bathgate, 13 miles away. Undaunted, a week or so later, he was even said to have attempted to run to Stirling and back – a round trip of at least 20 miles! Perhaps the greatest follower in my footsteps, however, was Mike Ryan, a young pupil at St Modan's High, when I returned to teach there the following year. Later emigrating to New Zealand, he was to go on to win both Commonwealth and Olympic bronze medals in the marathon.

Two of these sports forums were memorable for me for very different reasons, however. The journey in the dark to and from Oban was a nightmare. I am not a good passenger and, jammed in the back of the small car with Dunky Wright, I felt dreadfully sick on the way north. Luckily, I revived when we reached the Gathering Hall and was able to perform satisfactorily, but, on the way home in the early hours of the morning, the driver suddenly announced that the petrol gauge was registering empty and he had no idea where we could find an all-night garage. The thought of being stranded in the blackness of a Highland road compounded my nausea. There were no mobile phones then! Somehow or other, however, the car managed to limp the next 15 miles to Stirling where the blessed lights of an open garage appeared.

The journey home from Galashiels was almost equally nightmarish. Even today the first half of the road up to Edinburgh is notorious for its tight bends on the hills mile after mile. That night a dense fog descended just after we left Galashiels and we had to crawl at a snail's pace, trying to use the grass verge on the left of the road as a guide. There were no kerbs! Suddenly, as we crossed the borderline into Midlothian, the middle of the road magically lit up as our headlights caught the line of cat's eyes and we were able to speed up. Then, within a few miles, the fog lifted as dramatically as it had descended and we coasted down into Edinburgh in beautiful moonlight.

These sports forums produced one rather irritating and unpleasant side-effect, which shows how different were the attitudes to 'amateurism' then compared with the complete laissez-faire of today. I received a letter from the SAAA demanding to be informed why I had not asked their permission to attend such functions. They went on to ask what fees I had been receiving and requested also a note of my so-called expenses. I wrote back at once that I had received not a penny and, as regards expenses, I had usually been taken by car and, indeed, was then actually 17/6 out of pocket for a taxi. I pointed out, too, that my appearances had in fact been a distinct asset to the sport, encouraging young people to take it up (cf. Tommy Malone!). Then, tongue-in-cheek, I formally asked their permission to continue to speak to schools, youth organisations, sports clubs, etc. The laughable result was that they, obviously missing the sarcastic tone of my reply, wrote back solemnly giving me their permission.

To revert back, however, to the events of this hectic tenth week, on Wednesday, 20 October, I attended the Sports Forum in Paisley and, on the Friday, I was guest of honour with the Chief of Air Staff, Air Marshall Sir William Dickson, at a lunch in Turnhouse. I had already informed Wing Commander Duncan Smith, my CO, that my three-year period of active service would be completed in January and he had been trying to persuade me to accept a permanent commission – really a rare and distinct honour as only about one in a hundred short-service commission non-flyers were given such an offer. He now decided to put the pressure on by remarking on my circumstances to the Air Marshall, who turned to me and asked, 'What do you think about life in the service?' I was embarrassed but was then inspired to the diplomatic reply, 'I think there's no life like life in the RAF, sir!' This eventful day was still not finished as I had to dash off early from work in the afternoon to act as guest-chairman at Hamilton Swimming Gala in the evening. Fortunately, I had managed to fit in a ten-mile road run before attending the lunch.

The 11th week after Vancouver, the last in October was certainly my busiest yet in terms of the number of places and events I visited. Simply looking at the list of them all now makes me feel exhausted:

Monday: Bathgate Rotary Club lunch and Baillieston Youth Clubs in the evening

Tuesday: Motherwell Sports Forum in the evening preceded by tea at Margaret Girvan's (swimming gold medallist)

Wednesday: Dollar Academy in the afternoon

Thursday: Kirkcaldy – Children's Week – evening

Friday: Bridge of Allan – St Modan's Dinner Dance

Saturday: Celtic Park – guest at Celtic v. Falkirk match, including broadcast on internal link to Belvedere Hospital.

The list clearly shows my increasing difficulty in juggling the demands of work, training and social events. Moreover, I did not drive at this time and was heavily reliant on public transport – which was even more time-consuming. Nevertheless, I still managed to train every day of this week, totalling 66 miles, but no run was longer than ten miles. I simply had not the time to run farther and, looking back now, I wonder where I got the energy from! Yet on the next day, the last Sunday in October, I still managed to clock my fastest training time (2hrs 49mins 15secs) for the 25-mile Slamannan/Castlecary course (a very hilly one).

This week concluded the year, which I have been chronicling in some detail, describing my preparations for the Empire Games and its aftermath. From 1 November 1953 to 31 October 1954, I find that I had run almost 4,000 miles (3,977½ to be exact) and this despite at least two complete weeks in May and August and other odd days when I was unable to do any running – not too bad a total for a spare-time athlete!

I had still one major function to attend, however – Shettleston Harriers' presentation to me. They had deliberately delayed until after Falkirk Town Council's presentation and that evening I saw why. Lord Wheatley, the eminent judge and a Shettleston Harrier in his young days, handed over their gift – a large silver salver to complement the tea service that Falkirk Town Council had given me. It was inscribed:

PRESENTED to
JOSEPH McGHEE
By FELLOW MEMBERS of
SHETTLESTON HARRIERS
In RECOGNITION of his WINNING
EMPIRE GAMES MARATHON 1954

I was also made an honorary life member of the club.

My last presentation was, perhaps, the most surprising of all. The following February, I was invited to a packed Sunday evening gala concert in St Andrew's Halls, Glasgow, by the Celtic Supporters' Association. Top of the bill was that droll comedian, Chick Murray, accompanied by his tiny partner, Maidie. Then, along with Dick Currie, the Empire and Commonwealth Games flyweight boxing champion, and the footballers of the year, I received a large silver cup inscribed simply:

PRESENTED TO
JOE McGHEE
EMPIRE GAMES (1954) MARATHON WINNER
FROM HIS ADMIRERS
20-02-55

Chapter 7

Changing Careers

AS WE entered November 1954, I was faced with a momentous decision – whether to accept the offer of a permanent commission in the RAF or to return to schoolteaching. The whole direction of my future life depended on my choice now. My mind, however, had really been made up for some time when I finally presented myself in the CO's office with my papers of departure ready for his signature. The interview did not last long. As he scrawled his signature, he grunted, 'You bloody fool! What can you expect to become in civvie street? A mere headmaster!'

In one way, of course, he was right. A career in the service clearly had distinct advantages. My next promotion would have been to squadron leader and, at my age, the future prospects might have seen me climbing much higher up the ladder. From the point of view of my running, too, even at present I was my own boss and could virtually arrange my timetable to suit my training. On the other hand, however, my next posting, already overdue, would almost certainly have been an overseas one, and problems of climate, opportunities to compete and facilities to train might have brought my athletics to an abrupt end.

The truth was that I had been thoroughly spoiled by spending almost three years at Turnhouse. Early in my posting, I had been given permission to 'sleep out' at my home in Falkirk and, in my last year, owing to a shortage of accommodation in the officers' mess, they had asked me to 'live out' (normally restricted to married officers). They even paid me extra living-out allowance despite the fact that they were not, in fact, gaining an extra room. The mess secretary had long since unofficially put my name opposite the TV room on the accommodation list! I was thus able to enjoy all the social activities of home and participate in all my athletic club events!

The only snag was the frequent spells as orderly officer when I had to stay overnight at the airport. These duties fell to the lot of the comparatively small number of junior officers and their pattern was not regular, averaging out one every eight or nine days. (Our station had a much higher proportion of senior officers as it was the base for Headquarters 66 Group Coastal Command as well as 603 Squadron, 12 Group Fighter Command, to which I belonged.) The duties during the day were not onerous but at night when the airport shut down I found myself in virtual sole command. I had to inspect the guard and any prisoners in the guardhouse at least once after midnight and then accompany a corporal dog-handler in a jeep to the opposite side of the airport to check on the Ferranti facilities. Then I used to dive back to bed again! Only twice, however, was my sleep really seriously impaired by these duties. Throughout one night, I had to decode a series of messages informing us of my previous CO's death in a car accident in Germany. These included one of sympathy from the Queen. Then on another night, I found myself trying to prepare for a forced landing by a plane in difficulties. Luckily, it found sanctuary elsewhere! Though my training schedule could be interrupted by such events, my main complaint was social. I grew to resent not being able to plan my home activities with any certainty. Early on in my posting, I even volunteered (unsuccessfully!) to act as orderly officer once every week as long as it was the same day and night. After my return from Vancouver, however, I managed to wriggle out of even this duty. When asked in the mess by the Air Commodore, 66 Group, with whom I had had very little previous contact, how I managed to fit in my training, I risked mentioning my orderly officer problem. He then promptly arranged to have my name removed from the duty roster.

Schoolteaching, of course, had considerable disadvantages from my present situation as I would be bound by a rigid timetable and would have to fit my running round it. I would need to do my long distances after school ended in the late afternoon and I planned also to fit in a fast 3½ to 4 miles during my lunch hour, though I was later to discover that lunch supervision duties might interrupt the latter. Luckily, one or two of my younger colleagues generously volunteered to do my stint in order to help me keep my training schedule unbroken. I was to find, too, that the burden of work was much heavier than I was used to. In St Modan's, I was expected to correct a major ink exercise for every pupil in each of my classes every week – and I had 54 pupils in one class (1A) alone! It has been well said that 'the epitaph of the English teacher is "he did his corrections"'. I remember coming home one evening the following year laden with a bundle of exercise books and, in sheer frustration, hurling the lot everywhere across my bedroom!

Nevertheless, my mind was definitely made up. I had enjoyed my brief term's teaching in my old school, St Modan's High, Stirling, before entering the RAF and

I wanted to return there. A big attraction, too, was that I would be able to train over the countryside where I had first begun to run. I therefore applied to Stirlingshire Education Department and was appointed as assistant teacher of English in St Modan's. I was back for only two weeks, however, and was just settling in when I was informed that the headteacher of Stirling High School had requested my services. I reluctantly agreed on condition that it would be a secondment for only a term. In fact, I was to enjoy thoroughly my spell in the old High School up on the Castle Rock. The rector welcomed me most enthusiastically, telling me that he believed in members of his staff having achieved distinction in other spheres as well as academically. He himself, indeed, was a top marksman. The boys, too, were equally as enthusiastic and I soon had packs of over 50 boys running regularly along the Back Walk of the Castle Rock and then down the crags and across to the King's Park where we would complete a circuit of the old racecourse. My own training did not really suffer as it meant adding only a mile extra to the 10- or 15-mile routes I had planned to run after school from St Modan's back to my home in Falkirk.

1955, then, saw me, of necessity, having to tackle a very different training regime, but I was never to regret my decision to leave the RAF. Despite all the drawbacks, by returning to St Modan's, I was to experience the greatest and happiest event of my life. It was there, almost a couple of years later, that I first met Margaret Law, the lovely young golden-haired domestic science teacher, a Stirling girl, who afterwards became my wife.

Meanwhile, my now more restrictive lifestyle at the beginning of this year finally forced me to refuse the various invitations to give talks. I made two exceptions, however. The first was the dinner organised in my honour by my old friends from Glasgow University Hares and Hounds with whom I had run for five memorable years from 1946 to 1951. The other that intrigued me was an invitation to speak at a Burns Supper in Falkirk at the BBC's Westerglen Club for which, obviously, a very different type of speech was required. I decided to risk the challenge, which I was to repeat on another two occasions in later years, but I shall leave the descriptions of my experiences at Burns Suppers to a later chapter.

Chapter 8

1955 – A Year of Success

(Second Scottish Title and Record)

1955 WAS, perhaps, my most successful year in road and cross-country running. It certainly was my best-ever season road running from the point of view of both the number and quality of my victories. In fact, I remained unbeaten throughout and set my best times for various distances. In running cross-country, however, though I ran my fastest-ever races, I had mixed fortunes, probably on account of the nature of my training. All my training was done on road and, consequently, I suffered in cross-country races when I encountered plough, mud, slippery uphill stretches and, above all, fences.

As I settled into my teaching job, I soon established a regular routine of training and ran in all weathers. On the Sunday, I would undertake a very long easy run (up to the full marathon distance) from home. During the week at school, I ran four or five miles every lunchtime. After school in the late afternoon, I would run home on alternate days via Denny and Bonnybridge to extend the distance to 15 or 16 miles. On the following afternoons, I would have to carry my clothes from the previous day home by bus, but, before doing so, I would run 10 or 11 miles on a lonely road circuit up past the reservoirs in the Denny hills and then back to school. Saturday afternoons were reserved for club runs or races – in winter over the country and in summer on the road at the various Highland Games. I never regarded these races as ends in themselves and, indeed, in order to maintain my mileage, I would often run for about five miles from home on the Saturday mornings even on race days. I aimed to total at least 100 miles per week.

The new year began, as always, with the Nigel Barge Memorial Trophy Five Miles Road Race at Maryhill on the first Saturday. I had never finished far up in the places in all my previous attempts at this event but this time I surpassed myself by recording my first win. Running neck and neck with Eddie Bannon, the Scottish cross-country champion, with 300 yards to go I was not surprised when he suddenly broke away. Quite content to finish second, I was galvanised into a sprint by the shouting of the crowds and the sound of feet pounding behind me. Smith of Plebian Harriers, the Scottish mile champion, was coming up fast and I decided to fight him off. Ahead of me, Bannon, chest thrust out, was relaxing prior to breaking the tape and I suddenly realised that I could take him – on the very last stride – the best possible place to pass a man as he cannot come back at you!

Less than a couple of hours later, I was being interviewed by Dunky Wright on the sports programme of BBC Scottish radio, and, waiting our turn to sit before the microphone, I was fascinated to see the hurly-burly of the editing of football results and reports even as they were being broadcast live in the tight little studio. Some of the minor leagues were ruthlessly omitted even as the reporter read and we were allotted a precise number of seconds for our brief spot.

The cross-country events of the next couple of months followed much the same pattern as the previous year. I finished in my usual fourth place in the Midland Championship at Lenzie on 29 January, improved to third place in the Inter-District race and International Trial at Millerston on 5 February, and then at the end of the month achieved my best placing – third – in the National Championship on Hamilton racecourse. I was consequently selected for the Scottish team for the International Championship in San Sebastián, Spain, in March.

I was determined this time not to miss the entertainment laid on by our hosts on the day before the race, and Eddie Bannon, our team captain, and I managed to attach ourselves to the party of officials setting out by bus into the Basque countryside. We visited the impressive basilica at Loyola, dedicated to the memory of St Ignatius, the founder of the Jesuit Society, and then toured the Basque hill country. Here, in a little town, we were entertained in the cobble-floored town hall to a fantastic display of bare-handed pelota. The players, who had pickled their hands, used them instead of bats to hit the ball. I picked it up. It was as solid and hard as a rock! A group of the townsfolk then went on to demonstrate an amazing feat of strength by harnessing themselves to an enormous stone block, lifting it up and staggering with it from one end of the hall to the other.

Arriving back in San Sebastián, Eddie and I decided to do some shopping for souvenirs. He surprised me by stopping before one window full of baby clothes and then walking boldly into the shop. He hadn't a word of Spanish and I knew that my grasp of the language was totally inadequate for purchasing the tiny garments he had in mind for his second child, who had been born not long before. 'I can get along by pointing,' he told me confidently, but he was taken aback when the young assistant shook her head vigorously and promptly disappeared. She returned almost immediately, accompanied by a number of other assistants who all stared at us. Obviously none of them could speak English; so I hesitantly tried French and Eddie managed to buy a few little things. Then one of them asked me why we wanted baby clothes. I replied, stressing that Eddie was the parent. They all at once broke into giggles and a further flood of Spanish as they explained to even more assistants who had just arrived to join in the fun. Eddie anxiously asked me what they were saying. When I replied that they thought he looked far too young to be a father, he beat a hasty retreat, leaving me to thank them!

My memories of the actual race the following afternoon, however, are not nearly so congenial. Indeed, they are mainly bad! The Scottish team packed well but far too far back in the field after the mad rush of the start. An amazingly large crowd of 30,000 lined the rails of the racecourse and, as we plodded past within touching distance of them, we were assailed by the garlic-laden breath of the spectators and astonished and amused by their chants of encouragement – not the expected, 'Escocia!' or, 'Scotland!' but, 'Whisky, whisky, whisky!' We certainly needed some! I was so disappointed by my eventual placing – a sorry 54th – that I threw myself face down on the turf after the finish. Immediately I became aware of a blanket being thrown over me and I had to fight off the attempts of a couple of Spanish soldiers who tried to cart me off. I wasn't in the least exhausted – only disgusted by my performance!

All my training from now on was directed exclusively to my main objective – the Scottish Marathon Championship in June – and I refused to be distracted by entering for any intervening races. After all the hullabaloo after my Vancouver win (I still held the title of 'Athlete of the Year'), I simply could not afford to slip up in this year's championship.

Meanwhile, I became involved in organising the youth side of the sport. Falkirk Town Council, having made a personal presentation to me, also gave me a large silver cup, which they engraved 'The McGhee Trophy'. This was to be given annually for some event that I had to decide upon. My first thought was to hand it over to one of the local athletic clubs to set up an open senior road relay race on the lines of the McAndrew Relay, which Victoria Park AAC organised in Glasgow at the beginning of October every year. No one to whom I spoke, however, seemed keen on the idea. The main drawback, perhaps, was that it would mean adding another event to an already fairly full national fixture list. I decided, therefore, to inaugurate a new event for schools, the Stirlingshire Schools Cross-Country Championship, and to organise it myself – at least on the first occasion.

I did not realise just how much work was involved both prior to the event and on the day itself. Inspired by Joe Walker's ideal of getting as many boys as possible to compete, I contacted the nine or ten secondary schools in the shire and asked them to enter teams of four boys (three runners to count) without any restriction on the number of teams they could submit. This idea was not entirely successful. Some schools certainly submitted several teams, notably the two with which I was personally connected, St Modan's High and Stirling High, who between them entered over 80 boys. Other schools, however, sent only their top four runners. With hindsight, in order to lessen the effect of pot-hunting, I should have asked for single teams of nine runners with six to count (the system I had experienced in the National Senior Championships, the Inter-Universities and the Inter-Services races).

I organised the race at St Modan's over the field of the Battle of Bannockburn and I wrote into the constitution the rule that the winning school should organise the following year's race and provide the team and individual medals, which I donated for this first occasion. The weather was beautiful and among the several dignitaries attending were Joe Walker and George Dallas of the National Cross-Country Union of Scotland. The county director of education, Mr W. J. Goldie, started the race and Provost Watson of Falkirk presented the medals. The trophy was won by a very strong Falkirk High School four with the first team from St Modan's High taking second place. The next year, I duly helped out with the race at Falkirk High who again won the trophy. However, on my moving to Midlothian in 1958 to become principal teacher of English at Dalkeith St David's High School, I lost contact with the event and have never heard what became of the trophy since. I have often wondered about its whereabouts. Is it lying, perhaps, in some school's trophy cabinet? It should never have been kept by a school no matter how many times they might have been successful. If the event had been abandoned, then the trophy should have been returned to Falkirk Town Council.

I also became involved that May with the County Schools' Sports held at Brockville Park, the home of Falkirk Football Club, where I inherited Joe Walker's former role as official starter. I'm afraid, however, that my neutrality as an official was rather embarrassingly compromised when I was snapped cheering on my own runner, young Pat Flaherty, who against all expectations won the Senior Half-Mile! Though I was involved both morning and afternoon at the sports meeting, I was determined, nevertheless, not to let my own training be interrupted and, in fact, I managed to run from the football ground's dressing rooms at lunchtime on a ten-mile road circuit that took me out beyond Bonnybridge.

I was able, therefore, to maintain my regular mileage in training without any of the interruptions that had troubled me the previous year before the championship. I did not even attend as a spectator the early season road races, such as the Glasgow to Alexandria race, to note how any of the potential contenders for the championship were progressing. Indeed, on the Friday evening before the marathon, when I settled down to a jigsaw puzzle in an attempt to relax and calm my nerves, I had no idea of who would be lining up with me the following afternoon.

The next morning I was shocked and very much annoyed to be handed a copy of one of our popular tabloid newspapers, which had devoted almost its whole back page to a supposed interview with me under the banner headline: 'The Forgotten Man Hits Back'. I was even more shocked when I read on and found myself declaring that I was going to set a new record that afternoon. A sub-heading then proclaimed 'Not Superstitious' and quoted me bragging, 'I'm not superstitious. They can give me number 13. I'll show them!' I did not even know that my number was to be 13 until I arrived at the start! As for asserting that I was going to beat the record, I would never at any time state that I was even going to be able to finish the 26 miles. I had found to my cost (and I had also witnessed the fate of so many others) that you could be running on top of the world at 20-odd miles and yet be reduced to a shambling walk within the next half-mile if the dreaded 'knock' hit you. Obviously, this sports reporter had obtained an advance copy of the programme and based his entire supposed interview on it. I later tackled him when he attempted to speak to me afterwards and I demanded to know why he had fabricated his story. He cheerfully admitted the practice but defended himself on the grounds that he had been correct in his predictions. I had, after all, won the championship and broken the record!

When we lined up across the main Falkirk to Edinburgh road, just beyond the Salmon Inn Brae junction, I recognised not only my regular opponents from past years but also some surprising and yet familiar faces. The latter might be new to full marathons but were, nevertheless, noted competitors over the country and at the lesser road distances. I had been toying with the idea of changing my tactics from last year's waiting game but now, just before the gun went off, my mind was finally made up. I determined to use shock tactics and set off very fast in an attempt to leave my opponents behind on the very first mile up the hill through Polmont. This was, perhaps, a sign of my growing confidence in my own abilities that I would not admit even to myself.

The ploy worked. I took them by surprise and both experienced marathoners and novices alike, with the thought of the miles ahead, soon fell back. Not long after the five-mile mark at Linlithgow Bridge, my dad, sitting in a car driven by Duncan O'Hara, a headteacher friend of ours, shouted that I had a lead of more than half a minute from the leading bunch behind me. Ignoring my own official times, I kept hammering on. I was intent only on receiving from my dad information about the nature of the gap between the next runner and me. It gradually increased to over a minute by the ten-mile mark at the foot of the hill up into Winchburgh and then neared three minutes by the 15-mile checkpoint at the Boat House Bridge, a mile west of Turnhouse airport.

The whole marathon course was familiar to me not only from my experience of the race two years before but also because I had often run this road in reverse back to Falkirk when I was in the RAF. Now, as I rounded the perimeter of the airport to reach the Glasgow to Edinburgh road, and then on to the Maybury junction at the city boundary and down to the Barnton crossroads, I was on my former daily circuit from Turnhouse and running freely. About half a mile uphill from Barnton, I passed the 20-mile mark and found that I had extended my lead to over five minutes. Even if I was beginning to feel the pace, those behind must be feeling it worse! Thus encouraged, I pounded on. Allan Scally told me afterwards that he was astonished when he heard my times announced in the stadium. I had run each of my ten miles (just over 52 and 53 minutes) faster than some of his own times in winning the World Professional Ten Miles Championships.

As I passed the Telford Road/Queensferry Road junction and was heading downhill on to the long stretch of Ferry Road, my dad yelled that the nearest runner had just dropped out at 21 miles and that I was literally miles ahead of the rest of the field. The news encouraged and relaxed me at what was always a critical stage in this race and I continued running easily into Leith. Nevertheless, though I knew that I was so far in front, I still wanted reassurance of the gap and would not let my dad go on to the stadium as I toiled up the last half-mile slope back towards Meadowbank. Indeed, he almost missed my finish!

I entered the track by a gate in the north-east corner of the stadium and had to cover about 120 yards before starting a complete 440-yard circuit to the finish. In a mood of sheer exhilaration, I sprinted beaming through the tape and Allan timed me at 64 seconds for that last quarter-of-a-mile lap. Even then, I had no idea of my overall time. When the official timekeepers informed me that it was 2hrs 25mins 50secs (faster than any Olympic winner's time before 1952), I was astonished that I had broken my own last year's Scottish native record by almost ten minutes. It certainly seemed to impress the SAAA office-bearers. The previous year, after my Vancouver victory, they had given me the Coronation Cup for the Scottish Athlete of the Year. Now, they awarded me the Crabbie Trophy for the best performance of all the events in the Scottish Athletic Championships. Emmet Farrell, in his 'Running Commentary' feature in the *Scots Athlete* (August 1955) was lavish in his praise. Under the headline 'McGhee's Wonder Marathon', he wrote, 'One hesitates to use the term fantastic to athletic feats nowadays because standards improve so rapidly that superlatives cease to have much meaning but there can be little doubt that Joe McGhee's record-breaking 2hrs 25mins 50secs marathon was easily the feat of the championships and puts him into world class in this specialised event and, if I may say so, puts an extra glitter on his British Empire medal.'

I recovered remarkably quickly from my record run. My legs were, of course, very stiff and sore on the Sunday, but my cure being 'a hair of the dog that bit you', I forced myself out for a five-mile run. It was sheer torture to start with but, before I finished, I was beginning to move more freely again. Next day, I was back to normal and into full training again.

I certainly was not going south for the AAA marathon, now only two or three weeks away. I had no intention of taking the risk of competing in two first-class full-length marathons so close to each other. In those days of part-time training, no matter how apparently fit you might think you were, it was only when the going really got tough in the vital last four miles that you became aware of how much you had taken out of yourself in your previous effort and began to feel physically, emotionally and, even more, psychologically drained.

I was pleasantly surprised to see that the AAA marathon was won by R.W. McMinnis, a sergeant and former team-mate of mine in the RAF cross-country team. His time, 2hrs 39mins 35secs, almost 14 minutes slower than my Scottish time, encouraged me to hope for an invitation to represent Britain in some of the European marathons later in the summer, but, alas, no British vest came my way. Four Englishmen were chosen for these events despite my having recorded the fastest time for any Briton that year.

I should have remembered my experience after my Vancouver victory the previous year when, after Jim Peters was forced to withdraw from the British team for the European Championships, I had had a hope, admittedly faint, of being chosen in his stead. His place, however, was given to one of the Englishmen who had finished behind Peters and Cox in the AAA marathon.

I recall even tackling Jack Crump, then the kingpin of British officialdom, at an evening sports meeting at Ibrox Park later in the season, to find out why I had never been chosen for Britain. His reply: 'Well, we would always have the additional expense of bringing you down from Scotland,' amazed me! He had no answer to my indignant reply that in my service days the RAF would have sent me or even that now I would gladly have paid my own fares down to London. What a contrast this penny-pinching is to today's lavish expenditure on weeks and even months-long training and acclimatisation trips abroad!

One notable highlight of this summer of 1955, however, was the sports meeting held at Elgin City's football ground. It all began earlier in the year when I was contacted by an Elgin telephonist. He wanted me to help with some sort of publicity stunt to assist in obtaining funds for a roof for Pluscarden Priory, which the Benedictine monks had been gradually restoring. He seemed to think that my performing some kind of run at a five-a-side football competition, which he hoped to organise, would be enough. I offered to establish a time for running from Elgin to some well-known landmark and back. Forres struck me as being a suitable choice as the total distance, depending on the starting and turning points, would be approximately 24 miles – a useful training run for me.

My effort on its own, however, would not have been much in the way of a fundraiser and I suggested adopting the same idea as we had used at Fort William the previous year. Shettleston Harriers and St Bridget's Youth Club would call ourselves 'Lanarkshire' and compete against the athletes and youngsters of Morayshire. We would run only for points and no prizes (and hence no expense) would be involved. Everything seemed to mushroom from that and we finished up with a full-scale sports meeting including a five-a-side competition embracing Scottish senior football clubs with top teams such as Celtic and Clyde, that year's winners of the Scottish Cup.

One needless and ridiculous expense was incurred, however. The Northern Area officer of the SAAA insisted that a medical attendant should follow my road run all the way to Forres and back; yet I was running at least that distance and often more every weekend as part of my training!

The financial success of the venture (I think at least £400 was raised for the monks – quite a tidy sum in those days) was largely due to the dynamic and generous efforts of Mrs Blandford, who owned three distilleries in the area. She paid all the expenses so that every penny of the gate money was given to the monks and yet she insisted on donating a host of prizes so that every boy from Glasgow would return home with something. On meeting her in the arena before my event, I was astonished when she told me that she had set aside two tartan travelling rugs, one for me and the other for Eddie Campbell, the Ben Nevis winner, who was going to attempt the run with me. 'This one is in your tartan,' she informed me, 'but this other one is much better quality. Which do you want?' Needless to say, I chose the latter!

The meeting was blessed with glorious weather and a great turnout of spectators, but it was rather too hot for a long road run – with, moreover, a fairly stiff headwind on the homeward half. I warned Eddie that I would put on a show for the crowd by a fast start round the track and suggested that he keep up with me until we were out of the town but then run at his own pace. He agreed and then added, with a smile, 'I might not be finishing. Have you seen the medical attendant?' She was a young lady doctor!

I went off very quickly and soon left Eddie on the downhill, tree-lined stretch after we headed west from Elgin. Forgetting about the following breeze, I set, perhaps, too fast a pace on the outward half. When I reached the outskirts of Forres, I kept going for almost a mile before turning at the cross, which was near the far west end of the town. Heading back for Elgin, I passed Eddie who was just coming into the town and waved to him. Then I became conscious of the wind in my face and had a much less comfortable return journey, especially following the doctor's car on the last uphill stretch into Elgin, though I was still able to put on my usual grandstand finish for the spectators. Unfortunately, I don't have a record now of my exact time but it was nearer the 2hrs 20mins mark than I had hoped. Nevertheless, it wasn't too bad for what was essentially a training run for me and it seemed to impress the local crowd. Eddie later told me that he had dropped out not long after leaving Forres. He had hoped to be picked up by the young doctor but he was very disappointed when she simply gave him a couple of aspirins and got him a lift in another car!

As we were about to leave Elgin City's now almost deserted ground late that afternoon, I found a wooden case sitting at the edge of the grass. Opening it, I was surprised to see that it contained a large silver cup and, on reading the inscription, I was even more astonished to discover that it was the Scottish Cup, one of the most coveted trophies in Scottish football. My dad immediately realised that it must have been left there by the Clyde team who had brought it north to display it to the Elgin crowd. There was no sign of any of the footballers, however. Then my dad remembered that the Clyde team had been staying in our hotel the night before; so we decided to take the cup back to the hotel after tea. We were in luck. They had not yet left for Glasgow and no one had discovered that the cup was missing! They were greatly relieved, indeed, when we handed it over. I have often wondered since what would have happened if someone else had decided to go off with it. Still, I can always say that I once had possession of the Scottish Cup – even if it were only for an hour or so.

Two other events were to make that weekend an even more memorable one for us. Mrs Blandford had arranged, unknown to us, for a bottle to be placed in my dad's bed that Saturday night – a whisky bottle (and he was a teetotaller)! Next morning, she took us in her car to Mass at Pluscarden Priory, a few miles away. We were most impressed by the silence and beauty of the valley in which the roofless priory stood. Not long after we returned to Falkirk, I was delighted to receive an illuminated parchment from the monks, which stated that my name had been enrolled in 'The Pluscarden Kalendar of Everlasting Remembrance', which is kept in the sanctuary of the priory church and that I would be remembered at all Masses and in prayers 'at all times' in the priory. Almost a quarter of a century later, I was to return with Margaret and our five children to visit the now-restored priory and still marvel at the quietness of the setting.

I remained unbeaten in the lesser road races at the Highland Games that I entered – mainly in the central and eastern areas. These races were run on a handicap basis. Everyone started together but competitors were allotted so many minutes to be deducted from their actual finishing times. As a beginner to road-racing a few years before, I had been given the novice mark of half a minute per mile, thus totalling 7½ minutes in my first 15-mile race. When I began to win the handicap prizes and then later the scratch prizes in races, my allotted times were quickly reduced and for some time now I had been the backmarker running from scratch. Indeed, I was now running so well that, despite some runners having received many minutes of an allowance, I still had been able to win both the individual scratch and the handicap prize as well. Unfortunately for me, but in fairness to the other competitors, on those occasions I was not allowed to take both prizes but had to forfeit the handicap one. The actual prizes, donated by local businesses, were valued at only a few pounds and usually took the form of cheap clocks, barometers, cutlery or china – once even a suit-length of cloth from a neighbouring mill at Tillicoultry Games. Shotts Highland Games, however, also had a most unusual additional prize – a silver 15th century groat in a little presentation case for the winner of the 13 Miles Groat Race. It was the only time that I, as an amateur, ever won money! Nevertheless, it was certainly not the nature of the prizes but the thrill of winning the races that gave me most satisfaction.

I remember especially the 14 Miles Road Race at Dunblane Highland Games, the last Games of the year, held on a hot sticky day in early September. The local press reported that it had the finest long-distance field of any in Scotland that season and that I faced strong competition from other Scottish international runners. Nevertheless, I started off very fast round the track and set off north-west up the busy main Perth road in an attempt to break quickly from the rest of the field. My tactic was not as successful as I had hoped. By the time I had reached half-distance by Greenloaning and swung right back along the quiet road past the site of the Battle of Sheriffmuir, I could still hear at least a couple of pursuers only a few yards behind. I dared not look back. Indeed, in races I tried never to do so for such behaviour often acted as an encouragement to those following. Instead, I put in a fresh spurt until I could no longer hear the feet pounding behind. But how far had I gained? I dearly missed the presence of my dad in a car to give me information about the gap. Unfortunately, today we had not been able to fix up transport for him and he was anxiously waiting for news back at the Games' field.

My own increasing anxiety was effectively dispelled, however, about two miles from the finish when a cyclist suddenly shot past me on a downhill stretch with a cheery shout of encouragement. I recognised my young pupil, Pat Flaherty, who had won the county half-mile back in May. I had waved him on then and here he was repaying the compliment! I immediately spurted again. He was waiting when I turned on to the main road with less than a mile to go down to the field. 'You've got him!' he was yelling delightedly. Mentally, I was able to relax then and put in a furious finish. It is amazing how, once you know that you are certain of winning, your tiredness magically vanishes! My winning time for the 14 miles was a new record for the course of 1hr 12mins 7secs – ten seconds faster than last year. (Pat seemed to have caught the running bug now and would sometimes accompany me on my lunchtime runs at school. I remember one 4½-mile run with him the following frosty January when the pair of us, trying to pick our slippery way through Polmaise woods, lost the path and only just managed to get back in time for afternoon classes! When I later moved school, I lost track of Pat until 40 years later I was told at the press office in the Tower Hotel, the temporary headquarters of the London Marathon, that he had heard my interview on Radio 5 Live and was trying to get in touch with me. Unfortunately, though I tried afterwards to contact him, I was unsuccessful.)

The following Saturday, the last of this season's major races, the Scottish Marathon Club's 20 Miles Championship, was held at Cambuslang and was notable in that I recorded one of my best-ever times for the distance and yet, paradoxically, came so close to a really disastrous performance. This season, I had won both the Scottish Marathon Club's earlier races over the shorter distances of 12 and 15 miles. A win in the 20-mile race now would mean a clean sweep for me and obviously clinch the championship. I decided, therefore, to stick to the same tactics as had won me the SAAA marathon and other shorter races like last week's 14 miles at Dunblane.

Accordingly, I set a blistering pace from the gun and attempted to break away from the field. I succeeded: no one tried to hold on to me and, by the time I had passed the five-mile mark, I was running completely alone. Then, as I entered Hamilton, I began to feel distinctly uneasy and my stomach started to pain me more and more. I could not understand it. I thought that I had solved my pre-race diet problems years ago and I had taken only my usual lunch of egg and toast. I became aware, too, of the very sultry and humid conditions of the air and my queasiness increased. Determined not to show any signs of distress to my rivals behind, I nevertheless slowed my pace. The problem, however, grew worse and I knew that it could only be a short time before I was caught and passed. Unfortunately, I had not been able to arrange for transport for my dad, who was waiting at the finish, and I sorely missed his providing me with information and encouragement.

By this time, I had covered seven or eight miles and, having left Hamilton behind, I was now heading for Motherwell. Then, as I crossed the bridge over the Clyde between the two towns, it was almost as if a miracle occurred. There was a sudden crack of thunder, the heavens opened and the rain lashed down. Instantly, I was drenched and then almost immediately I began to recover. I felt as if I was running in a fresh, reviving shower. My tension relaxed and I increased to my full racing pace.

The rain didn't abate at all. The streets were soon awash as I circled back in the direction of Cambuslang and I splashed my way over those last 12 miles to the finish in fine style, my running strip plastered to my body, my hair slicked flat on my head and my face streaming with rain. I had never seen any of the other competitors after the opening miles. My time for the 20 miles – 1hr 45mins 9secs – astonished me, especially when taking into consideration my plodding pace during my bad spell in the second quarter of the race. My summer season had really ended on a high note!

As my winter season began, I now entered in earnest upon the most intensive and hectic training period in my life. In the four months from 2 October to 28 January, I never missed a day's training whatever the state of the weather or the way I was feeling. Indeed, this was, perhaps, the fittest time of my life. In these 17 weeks, I was never below 100 miles in any week and I logged a total of 2,112 miles, averaging over 124 miles per week. Twice I reached over 150 miles in the week, my biggest distance being 156½ miles in week eight from 20–26 November. In three further weeks, I ran over 130 miles and over 120 on a further six. Quite simply, I was determined to run more miles than anyone else – a principle that had brought me success so far and was now paying off in all the shorter races that I was running for my club in this period. These races, too, I must emphasise again, I was using simply as part of my long-term programme and I was certainly not keying myself up for them as ends in themselves. Bear in mind, also, that these mileages, which compare favourably with those of our full-time, subsidised athletes today, were being achieved at the same time as I was coping with the demands of a full working and social life.

The most important run of the week for me was the ultra-long Sunday one (on six occasions at least 25 miles) no matter what kind of race I had experienced the day before. For example, after recording the third-fastest time of 12mins 36secs for the 2½-mile lap when we won the Lanarkshire Road Relay Championship at Cambuslang on Saturday, 15 October, I ran over 30 miles the next day. In all these races, generally fairly short relays, I was producing fast times for Shettleston's winning first team. On these race days, too, I would run extra laps before the start and after the finish to maintain my mileage. At the above-mentioned Cambuslang Relay Race, in fact, I ran 4¾ miles before and five miles afterwards, and on 5 November, before the start of the Midland Cross-Country Relay Championship at Stepps Horse-Trotting Stadium, I ran three miles, then raced 2½ miles and afterwards covered five miles round the track.

Even in the *News of the World* Edinburgh to Glasgow Relay on 19 November, after a three-quarter-mile warm-up and then taking Shettleston into the lead on the second lap (the six miles from Edinburgh Maybury to Broxburn) in the fast time of 29mins 54secs, I got out of the competitors' bus at the beginning of the sixth lap and ran the seven miles into Airdrie before the race arrived, thus giving myself a total of almost 14 miles for the afternoon. Next day, I ran a 25-miler at an even medium pace in 2hrs 50mins 10secs to get rid of my stiffness and get myself off on a flying start that week to my longest weekly mileage of 156½ miles. I knew that I was improving on these ultra-long runs – as, for example, on 30 October I find myself noting 'slow-medium pace' for 28¼ miles and yet my time, 3hrs 5mins 40secs, was over 3 and 11 minutes faster, respectively, than my two previous runs over this course prior to my Vancouver win the year before.

I was taking risks, however, in mixing these cross-country races with my training, which was entirely on the road. The dangers of injury were all too apparent. On 3 December, for example, in the Lanarkshire Cross-Country Championship over six miles at Hamilton, won by Eddie Bannon, the Scottish champion, I negotiated the fences (my bugbear!) not too badly and, at the end of the first of the two laps, I was closing on the leading two, Bannon and Andy Brown of Motherwell YMCA, the Scottish ten-mile champion and a former RAF team-mate of mine when we won the Inter-Services Cross-Country Championship. On the second lap, however, Bannon broke clear over the broken ditches and I was catching Brown fast when I fell into a burn! I managed somehow to rally and began to close again on a tiring Brown but it was just too late and I finished third, five seconds behind him.

Though I was stiff and tired next day, I still managed to cover 25 miles in 2hrs 48mins 5secs and was back to running strongly and easily at the end. Yet the warning signs were there – I could quite easily have injured myself badly. Nevertheless, I was still to continue rather foolishly to ignore the risks. I suppose my competitive instincts were still too strong for my common-sense long-term approach. Indeed, two weeks later, on 17 December, I allowed myself, against my better judgement, to be persuaded into running the only six-mile track race of my life.

I had no intention of competing at all that day. I had, in fact, run 5½ miles in the morning at home before travelling after lunch to Glasgow to attend the SAAA meeting and presentation, where I received the Crabbie Trophy for the best performance in the championships and also the McNab Robertson Memorial Trophy for the third time as the Scottish Road Runner of the Year. Leaving the meeting, I decided to make for the track at Barrachnie in the hope of seeing the closing stages of the Shettleston Harriers Six Miles Track Championship. To my consternation, I found that they had delayed the start and were waiting for me. I had taken my kit with me with the intention of going out for a short run afterwards, so had no option but to strip there and then. As soon as I hurried to the start, the gun banged and I found myself in a race with no warming up whatsoever and with time for only a lap's easing off at the end. Nevertheless, I decided to go straight into the lead at once. Setting a fast pace, I managed to break from George Govan, the second runner, at two miles and then soon afterwards began to lap people. (The Barrachnie track was not the regulation quarter of a mile and we had to cover 29 laps plus a distance.) At four miles, Eddie Bannon caught me up and sprinted to pass me. I doggedly held him off, going flat-out for half a lap before finally having to let him past. Then I saw how spent he was and I immediately tried to pass him again on the inside as he had continued to run down the middle of the track. He at once veered in – too sharply – and half-tripped, half-stumbled on the edge of the kerb separating the cinder track from the grass. I was able to cut out round him and pass without too furious a sprint. My next lap had to be slow as I fought to get my breath back but I felt, nevertheless, that I was gradually pulling away from him. Then I recovered strongly to finish eventually half a lap ahead of Bannon, having now lapped all the other competitors. My time, 30mins 31secs, though slower than my more even-paced times for the distance on the road, was respectable enough, especially in view of the erratic bursts we had indulged in. Though I must admit I was pleased that I had now proved that I had the edge over Eddie on the track as well as the road, to me it was really a hollow victory.

The following day I certainly felt the effects of my efforts. Though I ran easily enough over my 22½-mile course, I was aware of a strain in my left leg and groin that was to persist until at least halfway through the week. Nevertheless, determined to run it off, I kept at it and managed to record 104 miles for this 12th week – my lowest mileage, however, since the second week of this winter period of training. I therefore resolved once again to stick more rigorously to my training policy of running only on the roads and avoiding short races whenever possible.

My next week's training began inauspiciously on Christmas Day when, owing to heavy rain and wind, I managed only ten miles instead of my normal long Sunday run, but, by dint of training almost twice a day that week, I brought my total up to 132¾ miles. I still managed, nevertheless, to keep up a normal social life. On the Friday, for example, I ran 10½ miles at lunchtime and then another 6½ at teatime before going to the Falkirk and Stirling telephonists' dance in the evening. The following day, Hogmanay, I ended the year in style with a run of over 12 miles in the morning and then, in order to increase my mileage for 1955, I went out again, running smoothly and easily, for another 15 miles in the dark of that Saturday evening – the only time I have ever run on a Saturday night!

Chapter 9

1956 – A Year of Disappointment
(Yet a Third Scottish Title in a Row)

NEXT DAY, I again achieved my usual New Year's Day's run of over 30 miles round Stirlingshire, finishing the 31½ miles strongly in just over 3hrs 32mins. I firmly believed, as I have stated before, that if I could run 30 miles in the depths of winter, I should certainly be able to race over 26 in midsummer.

Thus 1956 began well enough for me, though eventually it was to prove a year of very mixed fortunes. At the end of this first week of January, indeed, I broke my resolution about avoiding the shorter races and competed in the Nigel Barge Memorial Five Miles race – my excuse being that it was a road race and I felt, after all, obliged to enter as last year's winner. It turned out, however, to be one of my best-ever races, this time producing a new record for me.

My nearest rival this year was to prove to be Andy Brown from Motherwell. The two of us set a hectic pace, each striving to break the other. As soon as he would jump into the front, I would grit my teeth and hang on grimly to his heels, ignoring the distance. Then, as I sensed him slacking, I would reverse the process and take over the lead and he would hang on in his turn. We interchanged several times like this down the Switchback Road, round Canniesburn Toll and then back up Maryhill Road.

Approaching the right-angled corner at the cinema with just over 300 yards to the finish, we were racing absolutely neck and neck along the pavement. A crowd of spectators were lined round the kerb on the corner and I anticipated having trouble negotiating the tight bend at the speed at which we were running. I was on the inside of the pavement and, therefore, shortening my stride, I hugged the wall. Andy, on the outside, ran right into the line of spectators and came bouncing back, straight into my path. I was already braced for the impact, however, and took it on the shoulder. Then, realising that this was the psychological moment when he was still unbalanced, I at once broke into a long flat-out sprint for the tape and, having caught him by surprise, I won by at least 20 yards.

To my delight, I found that my time of 22mins 40secs had broken Ian Binnie's record by five seconds. My average time per mile was 4mins 32secs, but, to this day, I can hardly believe that I had kept up such a pace for five miles and I often wonder if the course was slightly below distance. On the other hand, however, I do know that, by competing against each other as we did, I had never run so fast before in a race of this length. Nevertheless, instead of heading at once for the Maryhill Baths like the other competitors to change, again in order to maintain my mileage, I ran another two miles, easing off, accompanied by Andy Brown. My example was catching!

Then, the following Wednesday afternoon, after receiving an urgent call at school, I was rushed from Stirling to Glasgow's Govan Town Hall where I was interviewed live about the race on that evening's nationwide BBC sports programme – the only Scottish item that week. It was very surprising for a Scottish road race (or, indeed, any English one!) to be featured like this and I wondered what football star or pundit had failed to appear that evening. Nevertheless, I had to admire Dunky Wright's livewire ingenuity in reporting and obtaining publicity for our Scottish races. We certainly don't seem to get the same coverage today.

I had been fortunate in suffering no apparent ill-effects from my strenuous efforts in this five-mile race and, despite the bitter cold, I was able to run 20 miles at a medium-slow pace the day after it. Therefore, as this was the year of the Melbourne Olympics, I now decided to try to intensify my winter routine of training by running 10¼ miles to school in the mornings and then from 12½ to 16 miles by roundabout routes back home again in the late afternoons. In addition, I still tried to maintain my lunchtime runs, though perhaps at a slightly slower pace than I had been accustomed to. This scheme meant that I could keep one set of clothes at school all the time. A helpful pupil who stayed near me in Falkirk carried my briefcase home with those dreaded corrections! I then began the very next day with this three-times-a-day routine and, on my second week of it, I logged my highest mileage of 153¾ miles.

My hopes of thus running over 30 miles a day at times did not last more than a week or two, however. It was not exhaustion that frustrated my plans. In fact, I was able to attend dances and other functions in the evening as well. I soon realised that I was not really a 'morning person', my best running being achieved later in the day. I disliked, above all, the chill of starting out on the dark frosty mornings, for, no matter the temperature, I always ran in shorts. I did try wearing a full tracksuit for a day or so but the discomfort of snow and sleet-sodden trousers soon made me revert to bare legs again. One morning, I thought that I had solved the problem of the cold by liberally coating my legs with Ralgex, a solid-stick embrocation, before setting off for school. It seemed to work well for I quickly worked up a nice heat in my legs soon after starting and I completed my ten miles in fine fettle. Then I went into the showers and immediately thought that I had scalded my legs. All that morning in the classroom they felt on fire!

What really ended my morning runs for good and all, however, was the day I found that a burglar had broken into the staffroom the night before and stolen the bag full of all my clothes! My situation would have been ludicrous in the extreme except, very fortunately, for the fact that, most unusually, that morning I had started feeling unwell after the first mile or so of my run and decided to turn back home and dress before catching a bus to school. The story of what might have been my dire predicament caused much hilarity among the pupils and inspired one wit to contribute a saga in verse to the school magazine. One stanza, I remember, began:

> *The janitor, ever an obliging chap,*
> *Lent him a barrel and a cap,*
> *And in that strange attire*
> *He ran round the shire ...*

The police eventually contacted me months later when I was at an International Schools summer camp at West Linton and insisted that I had to return to identify my clothes, which they had at last recovered. I was equally adamant in insisting that I could not possibly leave the 12 pupils from various Stirlingshire high schools, for whom I was responsible. I told them that my mother in Falkirk was perfectly capable of identifying my property and they grudgingly acquiesced. What I did not tell them was that my innocent pupils were all 17-year-old sixth formers! It goes without saying, too, that I binned the clothes as soon as I returned home.

Meanwhile, despite a continuing leg strain, I managed to total 129¼ miles during this last week of January, the 13th week of my four-month period of intensive training. It was to prove to be my last! I allowed myself once more, at the end of the week, to compete for Shettleston in the Midland Cross-Country Championship, at Woodilee Mental Hospital, Lenzie. This race had always been my bugbear and I should have learned from my experiences in the past. I ran 2½ miles in the morning at home and a three-mile lap of the course before the start. Though my time of 30mins 44secs was respectable enough for the six miles, I finished fourth yet again! This year, I made no attempt to hurdle the fences and, of course, lost valuable time going under them. Worse still, halfway through the second lap, I got caught on the barbed wire and promptly ripped myself off. I must say I suffered no pain – probably due to the adrenalin pumping through me – and, indeed, forgot the incident until I was washing myself afterwards when the blood began to flow. I found that my singlet had ripped diagonally from shoulder to hip and that I had a corresponding scar right down my back!

My despondency was somewhat relieved by an encounter as I was plodding back up towards the hospital buildings to change. I was stopped by a middle-aged man who earnestly inquired, 'What was the score?' I laboriously began to explain to him that it had not been a football match but a cross-country race and could not understand why my fellow team-mates were laughing. Then I glanced back down the slope to see a veritable kaleidoscope of coloured vests as mobs of runners (into the 100s!) stretched out behind me. It was no laughing matter for me the next day, however, as I suffered the onset of back trouble that was to plague me on and off for the next 25 years.

My main objectives this year, which I should have been absolutely single-minded in pursuing, were winning the Scottish Marathon Championship for the third time in a row – a feat that no one had ever achieved before – and then competing in the British Championship for selection for the Olympic Games. More immediately, however, I was tempted by the prospect of being chosen for the third time for the Scottish team for the International Cross-Country Championship and this meant that I had to compete in the Scottish Cross-Country Championship in about three weeks' time. I experimented with all sorts of heat and massage treatment, at the same time desperately trying to run off the pain in the short time at my disposal – to no avail, however. Nothing is more demanding for a runner than lower-back pain. On the morning of the championship, I was forced reluctantly to contact the club and withdraw from the race.

To my astonishment, the Association announced my selection for the Scottish team – an almost unheard-of honour as international selection without competing in the National Championship was virtually unprecedented. I had missed out, indeed, on possible selection at least twice before when I was in the RAF and unable to compete in the nationals. An innovation this year, too, was the arranging of special training runs for the team in Pollok Estate, Glasgow, on the two Saturdays prior to the international. I turned out for both of them and was able, despite my injury, to more than hold my own in the pack that covered the nine-mile course at almost racing speed. I was really forcing things too much; however, the pain persisted afterwards and I had to withdraw from the team midway through the week before they set off for Northern Ireland where the international was being organised this year. I still have the race programme, listing my name under Scotland. Three years later, however, I was able to win my way back into the team for Lisbon.

I now had less than three months to get fit again before the Scottish Marathon Championship. I travelled regularly to Allan Scally's home in Baillieston for massage and much-needed encouragement and I also sought help (quite often painful!) from a variety of sources – the physiotherapy department of Falkirk Royal Infirmary and private practitioners such as osteopaths in Marchmont, Edinburgh and Dalkeith. In the end, I won through (albeit temporarily!) simply by going out for long gentle runs, never pushing myself beyond the pain threshold and certainly not amassing the mileage that I had hoped for, but, nevertheless, I was able to join the line-up for the start of the Scottish Marathon in June over the same course as last year – Falkirk to Edinburgh.

Most of the regular marathon competitors were there. Nearly all of those competed in the Scottish Marathon Club's events and the Highland Games road-race circuit. I knew that I had nothing really to fear from them over the full marathon distance especially as the temperature today was unusually high. However, this year again, there were others who, though newcomers to this championship, were well-known competitors at shorter distances and these I eyed warily. In particular, I noted Harry Fenion of Bellahouston Harriers, a cross-country internationalist, with whom I had tussled in the past. He might be my biggest threat. I decided, therefore, to risk last year's tactics of going flat-out from the gun in the hope that, because of their lack of experience over 26 miles, these newcomers might be cautious in the early stages of the race. My plan was successful and I found that I had broken from the field in the very first mile.

As the race progressed through five and then ten miles, I didn't relax as my dad kept informing me about the leading runner behind, who was still shadowing me and within striking distance. As I had expected, it was Fenion. Nevertheless, the gap slowly widened until I had established a fairly substantial lead of approximately five minutes by the 20-mile mark near Barnton. Soon afterwards, Fenion dropped farther back and, I found out later, eventually retired at 23 miles. Meanwhile, running completely alone, I was left to face the last four or five miles along the Queensferry Road, down Telford Road to Crewe Toll and then along the Ferry Road to Leith. However, I was far from relaxed – indeed, I was more exhausted than at the comparable stage last year. My battle was no longer with the other runners but solely with myself. Ironically, I now realised that I was in a similar situation to that of Peters in the closing stages of the Empire and Commonwealth Games marathon. The parallel to the Vancouver weather conditions was striking. I had never encountered such heat in races in Scotland before.

I deliberately tried to keep a tight rein on myself and maintain my rhythm and breathing-rate even though my pace had become much slower. My dad's reports, however, were still very encouraging and I kept consoling myself, too, that those behind were feeling much worse. Nevertheless, I was very relieved to run down on to the Meadowbank track where I managed to produce my usual spurt to the finish and the welcoming arms of Allan Scally. I was rather disappointed that my time was just over 2hrs 33mins, but, on reflection, considering the appalling heat and my injury-stricken preparation, I suppose it was not too bad. After all, though almost eight minutes slower than my record, it was still the second-fastest time ever recorded in Scotland and almost 13 minutes ahead of the second-placed runner, my old friend and rival Alec Kidd of Garscube Harriers. I had, too, achieved one of my major aims of the year, my ambition of being the only marathon champion to register three wins in a row – a record that was to stand for almost 40 years.

I was interested to read the apt summing-up of that most knowledgeable athletics writer and marathon runner himself, Emmet Farrell, in the August 1956 issue of the *Scots Athlete*. Under the heading 'McGhee Comes Through Gruelling Test', he commented:

> Joe McGhee won the Scottish Marathon title for the third successive year, in itself a record sequence, and at the same time revealed a successful comeback after doubts occasioned by injury and delay. His 2hrs 33mins 36secs I consider most meritorious in the warm sultry conditions. Some criticism was directed against his extraordinary fast start in the heat and his very fast pace to the 20 miles mark (as fast as last year's record run) possibly provided Joe with more trouble over the last few weary miles than did his opponents. He probably was anxious and lacking in confidence at the start due to the break in his training.

It was only afterwards in the dressing room that I began to realise just how much I had taken out of myself. I was desperately thirsty and had taken no liquids since lunchtime, but, whenever I tried to drink anything, I was promptly sick. Indeed, it was almost three hours later, as I sat in the BBC studio in Edinburgh's Queen Street, waiting to be interviewed by Dunky Wright, that I managed finally to eat an orange. Weighing myself that night, I found that I had lost over 9lbs in that 2½ hours' grind in the afternoon, not a method of losing weight that I would prescribe for anyone, especially as I had drunk it all back again by the Monday following!

Because of my win, the SAAA selected me to compete in the British Championship the following month in Birkenhead. Though I wondered if this was allowing me sufficient time to recover, I felt I had to go ahead with the event as Olympic selection would be depending upon it. One important consolation that I did derive from my victory, however, was that my back trouble did not seem to have worsened and I was able to run fairly comfortably the following week. I then continued training without attempting to reach the mileages that I had been achieving at the turn of the year. In fact, for a fortnight that July, I had only short easy runs with a group of the senior pupils at West Linton, where I was attending the International Schools camp.

Halfway through my stay at West Linton, however, after much swithering, I made up my mind not to cancel my entry for a 15-mile road race at Aberfeldy and, catching an early bus to Edinburgh, I was in time to join the special bus taking Edinburgh athletes to the Games. This race proved to be one of the most enjoyable I have ever experienced.

Now 'enjoyable' is hardly an adjective I would ever apply to the experience of competing in any distance race, however exhilarating the feeling of euphoria after winning might be. As a fellow athlete remarked, 'It's like battering your head against a brick wall. It's pleasant once you stop!' The tension and feeling of weakness before the start, then the actual physical suffering in having to drive yourself on during the competition and sometimes even the bout of sickness at the finish – all this was a much more usual occurrence for me. (I'll discuss in a later section why I ever liked running at all!) Today, however, the entire experience was different.

On the crowded bus from Edinburgh, I had seen only a few fellow road-racers and none of them was likely to offer me stiff competition. In the marquee where we changed, however, there were a number of runners who were strangers to me. Scrutinising the starting-entry in the programme, I noticed an unusually high number of competitors with the novice handicap of 7½ minutes for the distance. Clearly, they were locals, but how experienced were they? Looking at the wear and tear of their shoes, I deduced that some of them at least had been doing quite a lot of training. I immediately decided to rely on my reputation and attempt to overawe them by a blistering start. My ploy certainly was successful. As the gun banged and I sprinted clear, I heard one of the newcomers mutter to his neighbour in the line-up, 'Oh, he's off! There he goes!'

Glancing round as I turned out of the Games field after my opening lap, I saw that I was already over 100 yards ahead of the others. I kept up this furious pace until I was safely out of sight round the first bend in the road. Then, running easily, I relaxed and headed west along the south shore of Loch Tay. It really was a lovely bright afternoon with a gentle cooling breeze off the water. I was struck by the quiet. Obviously no one was going to attempt to compete with me and I relaxed even more. Looking round me, I began to enjoy the beautiful mountain scenery – a new experience for me in a race!

As I reached the halfway point at the head of the loch and turned back along the north shore towards Aberfeldy again, I could see no one behind me. My enjoyment then continued to the finish. Best of all, I was suffering no after-effects and seemed now to have recovered completely from my Scottish Championship race. In fact, I was able to attend the dance in West Linton after I returned that Saturday evening. I thus began to become more hopeful of my prospects in the forthcoming AAA Championship.

The AAA Marathon Championship, however, turned out to be my greatest-ever disappointment. I was absolutely disgusted at the inconsistency in the selection procedures adopted by the British Olympic selectors and even more at myself in the way I allowed it to affect my own running. It had been understood that this year Britain would take three marathon competitors to the Melbourne Olympics and that, as in the USA system of selection, the places would go to the first three in the national championship. I knew that the competition would be fierce but, studying the list of entries beforehand, I felt confident enough that I would make it into the team. After all, I needed to finish only third at worst.

As we prepared for the start, however, I could see no sign of my two main English rivals in the huge crowd of runners. Then I spotted one of them leaning over the rail in the front row of the spectators. 'Is he injured?' I inquired from a fellow competitor. Imagine my consternation to be informed that he, like my other missing rival, had already been selected for the Olympic team on the basis of the results of the Polytechnic Harriers marathon back in May and both of them were obviously not going to prejudice their position by risking defeat in the British Championship! With the starter already calling us to the line, I felt utterly shattered. There was now only one Olympic place available and it was essential for me to finish first – or nothing! Even second place would not be enough.

With such a high-quality field, I had intended going back to the tactics I had used in my first Scottish Championship win and in the Empire and Commonwealth Games marathon – in other words, play a waiting game until the latter stages of the race. Now, psychologically, I had received such a devastating blow that, when the starter fired his pistol, I reverted blindly to my tactics in recent races and shot into the front, leading the field at a very fast pace round the stadium and out on to the road. It really was crazy of me to try to break clear from so many highly experienced marathoners so early in the race. So keyed-up was I, however, that I did not even hear the warning shouts of Allan Scally and my dad who were in an accompanying press car.

The inevitable happened. A small group of five runners allowed me to pace them for the first 11 or 12 miles and I grew more and more anxious as I sensed them crowding on to my heels. I knew that I was running really far too fast for the conditions – it was again a very hot day – and the sensible thing would have been to fall back into the pack and let someone else take over the pace. I slackened my speed but was then taken aback by how quickly the small group swept past me and, before I could tail on to them, a gap had opened up. At once I found myself struggling as I tried to speed up again.

Though I seemed to be falling farther and farther behind the leaders, I was still running completely alone ahead of the rest of the field. I should then have deliberately relaxed. I had, after all, plenty of time yet in which to recover and pick off most of those in front but I knew now that that all-important first place was beyond my reach. Then I began to suffer in a way that I had never experienced before in any of my races – even in those where I had been well beaten. My throat began to ache and become more and more constricted until my breathing grew ragged. It was reported that at 19 miles I was suffering from cramp and 'it was clear Joe was not going to recover in time and, acting on advice, he packed it in'. The distance was earlier and the decision, moreover, was purely my own! Of course, my distress was purely psychosomatic, brought on by the sheer frustration of it all, and, seeing my dad and Allan beside the road, I simply stopped, bent down and then climbed into the car. Within the next mile as we passed the leaders, my breathing had come back to normal and the throat pains had completely disappeared.

Back in the stadium, I felt even more frustrated to hear the time of the winner, H. J. Hicks – 2hrs 26mins 55secs – more than a minute slower than my Scottish record the previous year, which had been ignored by the British selectors. Even the time of Alain Mimoun of France, the winner at the Olympics later in the year – 2hrs 25mins 0secs – was only seconds faster. As I watched those following Hicks into the stadium, I was struck forcibly by the shocking state of some of them who seemed to have lost all control of themselves. One man even had tears streaming down his face as he lurched towards the finishing line. My depression deepened as I asked myself, 'Is this sport? Why are they punishing themselves like this?'

In my blackest moods in the months following, as I thought back over the whole episode, I found myself beginning to query the value of the sheer volume of time and energy spent per week in amassing the mileages that I as a part-time athlete had recorded. Surely, I would ask myself, there are so many more important things in life on which to spend my spare time? I knew, of course, that I could never stop the running I loved so much until I was forced to do so by physical disability, but I seriously wondered if I could ever again justify to myself the sheer amount of time and effort necessary to reach the top in world-class competition. Thus my four years of fairly intense training and competition, which I have been describing in some detail, now seemed to be ending on a distinctly low note.

Chapter 10

Post-1956:
Successes Despite Injuries

MEANWHILE, WITH the persistence of the back trouble that I had suffered earlier in the year, I was forced, whether I liked it or not, to cut out virtually all competition for most of the next couple of years. My time was more than fully occupied, however. I took on more extra-curricular activities at school, such as editing the school magazine, producing a school play for the Saltire Society in Stirling and accepting another stint of International Schools camp duties, and, above all (and most delightfully so!), I began courting Margaret to whom I became engaged in 1958. Later that year, too, I was promoted to a principal teachership in Dalkeith, which involved me not only in more work but also in much longer daily commuting.

Nevertheless, in 1958, with only a fraction of the training I had managed before, I tried one or two of the shorter road races, repeating my wins in Dundee and Aberfeldy and winning a new one at the Anster Games in Anstruther. Then in December of this year, the *English Athletic Review*'s report of the previous month's Edinburgh to Glasgow Relay referred to the fact that I had 'been away from running for some considerable time' and noted that

I had run my team from sixth position into first with the fastest time for the second lap (six miles) of 30mins 58secs. I could probably have obtained a much faster time if I had not been content to stay with the leaders once I had caught them up before putting in a fast finish over the last quarter of a mile. The following year, indeed, on the same lap of the race, with even less training, I simply kept on going past the leaders after I had caught them earlier in the race and, running completely alone, I clocked a much faster time and established a new record for the lap.

In 1959, in the throes of house-hunting prior to our wedding in 1960, I proved that I could still compete successfully with the minimum of training by finishing fifth in the National Cross-Country Nine Miles Championship at Hamilton and winning a place in the Scottish team (restricted to seven because of the expense) for the International Cross-Country Championship in Lisbon. Here, after a very cautious start, I gradually fought my way past runner after runner to record my best cross-country international placing, finishing in the first half of the field, fourth for Scotland, but still a rather mediocre 47th. As the course consisted of several fairly short laps out from the national football stadium and over what seemed like a corporation rubbish tip intersected by a series of ditches that looked more like open sewers, which we had to jump, I suppose I was lucky in not aggravating my back complaint! Needless to say, too, this was yet another international trip when the team were not even told by the officials about the hospitality laid on by our hosts for the day before the race – this time a visit to the coastal resort of Estoril.

Though my training was still minimal and competition in full-distance marathons was out of the question, nevertheless I was pleased to see that I had lost none of my former speed over the shorter road races – winning, for example, the *Musselburgh News* Cup for the 12-mile road race that summer and taking Shettleston into a winning lead in the Edinburgh to Glasgow Relay on 21 November 1959, with my best-ever six miles on the second lap to Broxburn to establish a new record of 29mins 29secs. The *Sunday Express* summed up this race as 'one of the most exciting of the long series, and the man who made it so was former marathon champion, Joe McGhee. Picking up in fourth place in the second lap, McGhee covered his six-mile stage to turn a deficit of 100 yards into a lead of 200 yards for Shettleston. Despite repeated challenges, his remaining six team-mates kept in front to win by 50 yards.'

In the early summer of 1960, prior to my wedding, my only significant run was a very fast last lap in the Aberdeen Students' Charities Relay from Inverness to Aberdeen. As I set out on the 5¾ miles up from Bucksburn to Marischall College in the city centre, I suddenly realised that, if I put in a storming finish, I might just be able to catch the last train south and thus save the organisers the expense of my hotel room for the night. Accordingly, I piled on the pace down Anderson Drive, then along Queen's Road and Skene Street and raced up to the Lord Provost in the college quadrangle with the message from his counterpart in Inverness. After posing hurriedly for the photographers, I rushed to the Imperial Hotel where I changed more quickly than I have ever done. Luckily, the hotel was fairly close to the station and I caught the train as the guard was blowing his whistle!

Thereafter, for a year or so, working on a new house and garden restricted my competitive running to shorter races in which, surprisingly, I continued to do well. However, a bad appendix problem, a later resurgence of my back trouble, further study at Edinburgh University and then a move to

Aberdeen with another new house and garden to break in meant that my running was frequently interrupted. After each setback, however, I found that I just could not give up my urge to run and I gradually built up my training again until I could cover more than 20 miles fairly comfortably, if rather slowly. I was determined, however, not to enter competitions until I reached a standard that I felt would do justice to my past achievements. Unfortunately, the onset of arthritis in my knees finally put paid to my hopes of competing again at the highest level, though luckily I was still able to manage easy running for quite a few years yet.

Looking back over that decade of the 1950s, I realise just how fortunate I had been compared to so many of my friends in athletics. I did, however, have some regrets that some of my greatest athletic ambitions, three in particular, were never to be fulfilled. The first was to tackle the 44-mile run from Glasgow to Edinburgh. I was inspired here by Dunky Wright, who, even though he had retired years before, had suggested accompanying me. I knew from reading of previous attempts pre-war that the record was well within my capabilities. Unfortunately, both of us postponed the attempt until it was too late.

My next ambition was to compete in the Boston Marathon – the nearest then in the number of competitors it attracted to the huge fields of today's city marathons. Here I was inspired by Allan Scally who had relatives in that part of the USA. Sadly, however, my own injuries and, later, Allan's untimely death, caused me to abandon this idea.

Perhaps the most disappointing of all for me was the frustration of my ambition to make an attempt on the world record for 30 miles (not then a very distinguished one compared with today's times) as I knew that I was capable of running quite a bit below three hours for the distance. I planned first of all to tackle the 30 miles on a tarred course utilising the perimeter track round Edinburgh's Turnhouse airport. Ten laps or so did not seem to be very daunting and the course could be very exactly measured. My proposal came to nought, however, when I was informed that my time would not be recognised unless I ran on a 440-yard track. The problem for me with this idea was a purely psychological one – the sheer monotony and the need, as I ran, to break down the distance mentally into manageable units. Imagine what I would feel like as I heard the timekeeper intoning at the end of my first lap, '119 to go!'

Nevertheless, I was still determined to have a go and I set about planning how I would solve the problem. I devised a simple system of using four large, coloured cards – red, green, blue and yellow – to signify each of the four laps of a single mile and 30 large, numbered cards to represent the miles. As I ran round each lap, two cards would be prominently displayed. Thus, for example, if I saw 'blue' and '9', I would know that I was on the third lap of my ninth mile.

I then planned to make my attempt on the cinder track at Ibrox, Glasgow Rangers' football ground. I hoped to start at noon on a matchday so that, as I was nearing the last critical miles, I would have the advantage of a large crowd spurring me on. Alas, before I could complete the necessary arrangements, I was hit by the back complaint that was to trouble me on and off for the next 20 years. At once, I had to cut down drastically on my training and, eventually, when I began to compete again in the latter half of the 1950s, I had to limit my distance in races to a maximum of a half-marathon.

PART B

*The Joys of Running –
Then and Now*

Chapter 11

Five 'Inspirers'

I HAVE met many athletes in my running career, such as former Scottish champions Charlie Robertson, Emmet Farrell and Harry Howard, who influenced me indirectly by their general approach to the sport, their tactics in races and, above all, their generous encouragement to me, a beginner. Five men, however, had a direct and very important influence. These were Joe Walker, Dunky Wright, Allan Scally, Arthur Newton and, of course, my dad, Willie McGhee.

Joe Walker
Joe Walker had perhaps the greatest influence on my running career for, without him, I would never have started running in the first place. In my primary school, St Francis, Falkirk, I had been absolutely hopeless at games and sports. The smallest and lightest boy in my class, perhaps I was rather looked down upon by the others as a 'swot' (eventually the school dux), though I would never allow myself to be bullied, having qualities of tenacity and often pig-headed stubbornness that no doubt stood me in good stead later as a marathon runner! One morning, for example, in the school playground, which we shared at

that time with secondary pupils, I recklessly lashed out in my defence at secondary boys at least four years my senior and immediately found myself buried under a mass of bodies. One of the bystanders, Neil Mochan (later a Celtic player and coaching assistant), took pity on me and, seizing me by the seat of my short trousers, pulled me clear. Unfortunately the trousers ripped and I had to be given a safety-pin by my teacher to hold them together! The only event in which I ever competed at my primary school sports meeting was the egg and spoon race – and not very successfully at that! In secondary school, especially in my later years, however, it was a very different story.

Joe Walker was the principal science teacher, acting deputy head and my fifth-form master at St Modan's High School, Stirling. It was during the war years, 1941–46, and he kept athletics alive in Stirlingshire, organising open meetings, inviting leading runners and clubs from throughout Scotland, and, above all, founding St Modan's AAC, a club by no means confined to former pupils of the school. Indeed, one of our most distinguished members was Stewart Petty, the Scottish half-mile champion, and an ex-Stirling High School pupil.

Joe believed strongly in getting as many lads as possible to compete, and, with Bob Brownlee, the principal mathematics teacher, he organised all our inter-house events on what was at that time a revolutionary basis. The highest points were awarded to the house finishing each race with the greatest number of competitors inside a pre-arranged time. So, as a completely unfit and untrained first-former, I found myself breathlessly toiling with what seemed scores of boys from every year in the school in the Three Miles Cross-Country Championship. My first encouragement soon after the start occurred halfway up the hill towards Bruce's Battle-axe Monument above

FIVE 'INSPIRERS'

Bannockburn when I passed a tall fourth-year boy walking along and advising all the youngsters round him to take it easy. Then I found as I splashed my way through the Bannock Burn itself that I was beginning to pass others more and more frequently. My greatest thrill, however, was to catch the school captain, a six-foot sixth-former, on the last field before the finish. I was exhilarated to finish within the time and be a member of the winning house, Ardchattan.

The only event in which I had any success on sports day, however, was the obstacle race when my small size enabled me to wriggle past most of the others under the pegged-down tarpaulin! However, I was dragooned into the four-lap half-mile race when again I was within the time for my age (3 or 3½ minutes) and part of the winning team.

This was the pattern of the years following – participating in the cross-country and the half-mile championships, in other words, only two runs per year and no training whatsoever! Though I gradually improved my finishing positions among the leaders, by no means could I be considered athletic. Indeed, when my dad visited the rector prior to my entering upper school, Mr Foxworthy told him that I could not be faulted academically (I had just become junior dux of the school) but that I showed little interest in sports and games.

Joe Walker was to effect the transformation. After trying unsuccessfully to interest me in the athletic club, at the beginning of my fifth year, he announced that he had entered me in the Youths' Three Miles Cross-Country Race at Motherwell 'to make up the numbers in the club team'. I shall never forget that race – the only race in which I ever came close to collapse at the finish! I was left completely behind and breathless in the mad rush of the 90 or so competitors at the start. The going soon became very heavy after the recent downpours and I gradually picked my way through the throng along the muddy banks of the Clyde. It was when I passed my team's leading runner, Stewart Petty, toiling uphill over the plough, that I began to realise that I was not doing so badly. Still, I had no idea of how far I had to go. I imagined that the finish was round every corner and I kept pushing myself till I finally collapsed in sixth place into the arms of our club coach, Mr Ewing. It was the only race in which I was so utterly spent and that includes the Vancouver Marathon!

Joe now tried once again to get me to come to the athletic club, which used the school as its base. At first, I was reluctant. I lived ten miles away and certainly, with the burden of my final year's schoolwork, I simply could not afford giving up the whole evening on Tuesdays or Thursdays. Saturday afternoon, however, was a possibility and I decided one day to try it. That first visit was an unforgettable one for me. In the morning, I had gone to Falkirk Baths and swum the longest distance I had yet covered – 30 lengths of the pool. Even with my cautious breaststroke, it was an exhausting experience for me and I shakily emerged from the water rather weak and headachy. Nevertheless, after lunch, I decided to keep to my plan and set out for the athletic club, but, in order to save the bus fares, I foolishly cycled to Stirling. Joe welcomed me and, without further ado, sent me out with the senior pack, paced by the club's two fastest runners, Davie Clelland and Eddie Philliben. Not only did I have to run farther than I had ever done in my life – over five miles cross-country – but faster too! Immediately afterwards, I had to cycle the ten miles home again. I felt as weak as a kitten as I toiled up that last hill from Larbert to Camelon – my bike, too, had no gears! After tea, I was still so exhausted that I went straight to bed where I at once suffered excruciating cramps and muscle spasms. No wonder! We had no such event as the triathlon in the 1940s and this, my first and only attempt to combine swimming, cycling, running and then cycling again (without any training too!) could have ended my athletic career before it had properly begun.

Nevertheless, the bug had got me. I was now considered the lead runner in the club youth team and was less reluctant when Joe persuaded me to participate in other youth races and inter-club runs. That year, I easily won the School Cross-Country Championship, the County Schools' Mile Championship and then the School Mile Championship, breaking the record in the process. The latter gave me the greatest thrill because it won me the Quinn trophy, which had been donated to the school by Joe himself in honour of Dan Quinn of Irvine. Quinn, club champion of the Eglinton and Garscube Harriers and cross-country internationalist, had been the winner of the Irish 'Olympic' or Tailtean Games Marathon in Dublin in 1926. He died as a prisoner-of-war in Japan. Joe was later to write in the *Glasgow Observer* in 1955 that 'possibly to this trophy is due McGhee's inspiration to become the athlete of the year'.

Joe then started encouraging me regularly not only at club level where I won the Youths' Mile, Two Miles and Three Miles Championships but he also prophesied a future for me in university athletics, saying that I might later be able to break into the university cross country team. Not only did I become Glasgow University's leading cross-country runner, winning my 'Blue' and eventually captaining the Hares and Hounds section, but I was also chosen five years in succession for the Scottish Universities international team, captaining the team in 1950.

In my last years at school, many of the upper school pupils would walk the length of Stirlingshire (at least 12 miles) on the Holy Thursday pilgrimage to seven churches. On some parts of the route I would walk with Joe listening to his stories of his visit to the Berlin 1936 Olympics, especially to his vivid description of the epic marathon between Ernie Harper and Kitei Son, the Korean running for Japan, the eventual winner and the first Olympic winner inside 2½ hours. Little did I guess that only a few years later, I would beat his time by almost four minutes!

Joe, balding and smiling-faced, was an enthusiast for the marathon, though not himself built for running 26 miles. Inclined in later years to plumpness, nevertheless he would run regularly over the roads round Stirling encouraging the other club runners whom he had enticed into road running. His own greatest ambition was to finish the Scottish Marathon in standard time and win the standard medal – an ambition that we were all delighted to see him finally achieve. Thereafter, he devoted his energies to organising and timing marathon running, helping to found the Scottish Marathon Club and becoming its president. On a couple of memorable and influential occasions for me, he invited me on the bus accompanying the Scottish Marathon Championship runners from Falkirk to Edinburgh. It was then that I became finally hooked on the marathon. At that time, competitors had to be over 21 before being allowed to run the full marathon distance, and I resolved that, as soon as I reached that age, I would enter.

Meanwhile, Joe's advice was invaluable in getting me started on the shorter road distances. 'Relax,' he would say, 'go out, amble along and enjoy the sunshine!' I had just finished my university final examinations and could not face the thought of turning out on the training sessions for track races and having a stopwatch put on my efforts. I used to envy the road runners, who seemed much more relaxed, and that summer of 1950 I decided to follow Joe's advice to forget pace and get a tan. In a couple of months, I found that I had logged over 400 miles. It seemed a lot at the time but was low compared to what I would achieve in the years ahead. Naturally, I thinned in the face and all my family thought that I was losing weight. In fact, I had put on a stone and a half – from nine stones to ten and a half – which was to be my racing weight from then on. Obviously, I had been building up my leg muscles without realising it!

At the end of that summer, I made a conscious decision to abandon track running and, encouraged by Joe, devote myself completely to road races. Though I was a respectable track runner at one, two and three miles, I knew that my lack of a finishing sprint would prevent me from ever achieving international success. Astonishingly, in later years, my marathon training was to sharpen up dramatically my times at the shorter distances and my finish, indeed, was to be one of my strongest points. One of my last track races was the following June (1951) when I won the Jordanhill College Three Miles Championship, beating the Scottish School of Physical Education runner, Wilson Simmons, the same ex-Stirling High School pupil whom I defeated in the Stirling County Mile Championship five years earlier.

My second place to Scottish Marathon champion, Charlie Robertson of Dundee Thistle Harriers, in the Tillicoultry Highland Games 13 miless, my very first attempt at a major road race, whetted my appetite. Early the following May (1951), another second place (despite a strapped-up ankle!) in the 16-mile race at the St Modan's AAC/Stirling Albion meeting, organised by Joe, encouraged me still further, and on Joe's advice I decided to make my debut at the full marathon distance in the City of Edinburgh Marathon on 8 September that year. I had still a lot to learn, however. It was announced back in Murrayfield that at Niddrie Mill, the 15-mile mark, the leader was 'J. McGhee, St Modan's, who had covered the distance in 1hr 29mins 25secs'! After that, heading back through Craigmillar to Morningside, I tired very badly in the heat but still managed to finish sixth in what was to prove to be my slowest marathon time, 2hrs 48mins. Yet I was not put off and I determined to run more wisely in future marathons.

It was about this time that Joe was promoted to an administrative examinations post based in Glasgow's Royal Technical College (later Strathclyde University) and moved his home to Glasgow. His leaving Stirling was perhaps one among several reasons that eventually prompted my joining the Glasgow club, Shettleston Harriers. He was still indefatigable, however, in promoting the sport generally. I remember, for example, when I was first posted to RAF Turnhouse in 1952, his inviting me to an evening panel in Alloa where I renewed my acquaintance with another friend and mentor, Dunky Wright, and also Eddie Bannon, the Scottish cross-country champion and my future team-mate. Joe, of course, was to see me off from Prestwick airport on my trip to the Empire and Commonwealth Games in Vancouver and then shortly after my return take me to lunch in Glasgow. He also came to Falkirk for my Windsor Road reception and presentation and officiated at the Scottish Marathon Club's presentation. Later, too, when I had begun teaching again in Stirling, he ran with me in an epic relay of runners from Glasgow to Perth to advertise a National Health campaign.

Joe was a popular and familiar figure officiating at road races, cross-country events and sports meetings throughout central Scotland and, always wearing his distinctive grey trilby, he could easily be spotted. Indeed, one of my typically vivid memories of him was in one of Glasgow's 'steamies' – those communal wash-houses, which provided handy changing and washing facilities on Saturday afternoons for the hard-up Harriers. Head thrown back in a hearty laugh, he was perched on top of one of the tubs drying himself. Then, wearing only his towel, he stuck his hat on his head with the comment, 'I feel dressed now!'

Dunky Wright

That well-known marathon runner and sports personality, Dunky Wright, also took an interest in me from my school days. He was the marathon winner in 1930 in the first Empire Games in Hamilton, Ontario, with a time of 2hrs 43mins 43secs. He also won the AAA marathon in 1930 in 2hrs 38mins 29.4secs and in 1931 in 2hrs 49mins 54.2secs. His best time, however, was in the 1932 Olympics in Los Angeles where he finished fourth in 2hrs 32mins 41secs. My first personal memory of him was seeing the fantastic end of the Scottish Marathon at Meadowbank Stadium soon after the war when he was pipped in a sprint finish by that other great pre-war Scottish marathoner, Donald McNab Robertson.

Dunky's contribution to the sport, however, was even more massive in his media work. He wrote for the *Scottish Daily Express* and the *Sunday Express* and broadcast frequently on Saturday nights on BBC radio, giving publicity even to local club events such as our own club races in Stirling. The first time he mentioned me, however, he called me Jim and then later Tom McGhee and, from then on, I resolved to give my name as briefly as I could as Joe McGhee when asked by the press. I knew that Joseph, or worse still J, would never stick! He made a point of speaking to me and giving me advice whenever I attended cross-country or track races. On one occasion, however, his advice misfired. I had finished third in the Midland Youths' Cross-Country Championship (by far the strongest Scottish district). Hamilton racecourse that day (25 January 1947) was basking in glorious sunshine, but the Scottish Championship on 6 March on Lanark racecourse saw a dramatic change in weather, the track being buried knee-deep in snow. Dunky advised me to let the leaders go on the first of the two laps, allowing them to break down the snow. With my fairly slight build, that second lap, however, was a disaster. Everyone ran in single file on the narrow trodden path and, to pass anyone, I had to plough through the deep snow at the side, eventually finishing seventh. Later that same spring of 1947, however, he was at hand when I won the Novice Mile at Glasgow University and also a place in the team to visit Belfast and Dublin. Running as a substitute in the three miles at Trinity College, Dublin, the last event, I was to win the race and the meeting for Glasgow by a single point. We were dancing eightsome reels in O'Connell Street that night! The following winter, 1948, Dunky invited me to an evening for 'Olympic hopefuls' at Ibrox indoor track and later to a similar event on the outdoor track at Helenvale prior to the London Olympics. I was then only a young student of 18!

When I started road running, he appeared many times and publicised my successes. I remember vividly how he appeared on 29 May 1954, at the start of the Scottish Marathon Championship from beyond the Cloch Lighthouse, west of Gourock, and promised that he would do his utmost to get the winner selected for the team for the forthcoming Empire Games. I described this race to Ibrox, my first championship win, in detail in an earlier chapter.

Of course, after my Vancouver victory, he wrote a full-page spread for the *Sunday Express* and came to all the celebrations after my return on 14 August. Ever a bit of a showman with a flair for getting things done, he even arranged for the two of us to fly a fortnight later from Glasgow airport, (as previously mentioned), in a tiny, open-door helicopter and disrupt the Cowal Gathering by landing in the middle of the arena. I must admit feeling rather precarious as we followed what looked like a toy train down the Clyde and flew across the rain-swept water to Dunoon. There he had me change hastily into my running kit and then, rather to my embarrassment, run a quarter-of-a-mile lap of honour before the cheering crowd.

Later that year, he was to appear with me on the series of sports forums organised by the *Daily Express* throughout the country and we shared some hair-raising car trips on the dark winter evenings. In subsequent months, too, he arranged several appearances for me on radio broadcasts and even a live spot on the national TV *Sports Reel* after one of my Nigel Barge (five-mile) wins. I could have seen him far enough, however, when, immediately after my third successive Scottish Marathon Championship victory (Meadowbank, 1956), he persuaded me to accompany him to the Edinburgh Queen Street BBC studios. It had been a broiling hot day, and as I mentioned previously I had lost over nine pounds in fluid. Nothing would stay down but I managed to tackle an orange just before we finally went on air at 7pm.

I have many other memories of the balding, dapper, little man with his short, pitter-pattering stride, competing, for example, not too seriously, in the National Cross-Country Championship or later shouting me on to a record run in the Edinburgh to Glasgow Relay. My last abiding memory of him, however, was on the Glasgow to Perth Relay run (which I mentioned when writing of Joe Walker). He confided in me then his hope that the two of us might attempt together the record for the 44-mile run from Glasgow to Edinburgh before he finally had to give up active running. Alas, he was to die with that ambition unfulfilled.

Allan Scally

Allan Scally was the man who helped me most when I had almost attained international standard. To me, too, he epitomised the essential friendliness of Shettleston Harriers. I first met Allan in the late 1940s when, as Shettleston Harriers' coach, he used to accompany his club members on their annual inter-club runs with St Modan's AAC at Stirling. At that time I was the only St Modan's runner able to take out Shettleston's fast pack, on one occasion nearly drowning a very irate John Eadie when we plunged through the Bannock Burn in spate! Later, Allan was most helpful and generous with his advice when I used to meet him in his capacity as SAAA starter at Highland Games. Never once, however, did he try to persuade me to join Shettleston Harriers. I did so entirely on my own initiative, approaching him at Bridge of Allan Games in 1952. There was absolutely no question of 'poaching' on his part as some disgruntled club officials averred.

I had several reasons for applying to become a first-claim runner for Shettleston – not least, of course, the attraction of training and competing with top-class runners such as Eddie Bannon, the Scottish cross-country champion, and being pulled on by them. As a member, too, of Shettleston's first team, perhaps the strongest in the country at this period, I had access to national and international events denied to me as a first-claim member of St Modan's AAC. In Stirling by then, I simply had no long-distance runners to accompany me on my training. The breaking point for me occurred one Saturday afternoon when I travelled the 11 miles to Stirling to train with one runner who then refused to go out on the road with me, preferring to kick a football about in the gym. I had to run a solitary ten miles before catching the bus back to Falkirk. I could have covered more than double that distance in the time that I had wasted travelling, by running from my home and saving the bus fares! I made up my mind then to join Shettleston Harriers, but I must emphasise again that my main motivation was to get Allan's help.

Despite some adverse criticism of my decision to run first-claim for Shettleston Harriers, I must stress that I never severed my connection with St Modan's AAC to whom I owed so much. The *Stirling Journal and Advertiser* (19 August 1954) made this abundantly clear after I returned from Vancouver. It quoted me emphasising: 'Make it clear that the Club [St Modan's] is my first love and I still consider myself as being a member.'

Allan had been a great professional track athlete, as 'Scally of Broomhouse' winning the World Ten Miles Championship in 1927, 28, 29, 31 and 32. He was also a noted and very successful fell runner. He would tell me how some of these fell runners would literally launch themselves past him into space on the way downhill, throwing caution to the wind as they went sliding down the scree! As there was always about half a mile of flat before the tape, however, his superior speed more than compensated for his more cautious and saner descent. He was an even more successful and inspiring coach in his later years, moulding many raw young novices into championship winners. Though a professional, he was the finest amateur in the true sense of the word I ever knew. He really loved the sport and unselfishly gave of the fruits of his experience to young and mature athletes alike. His work at Shettleston Harriers and St Bridget's Youth Club, Baillieston, was universally appreciated. Yet, ironically, because of his own earlier professional athletic achievements, he was never, to my knowledge, invited to accompany the international cross-country team even when, as in Lisbon in 1959, almost half of us in the Scottish team were Shettleston Harriers and the other runners he knew well.

I used to be fascinated especially by his stories of the old professional runners and the tricks they got up to! They made very little money from their running unlike our top 'amateur'(?) runners of today. What little they got was from betting on each other in their groups or 'schools'. Of course, most of them cheated and used pseudonyms, unless they were like Allan who was so far ahead in class and in the long distances he ran that such cheating would have been well-nigh impossible anyway. I shall describe some of their 'tricks' later when I discuss the differences from today.

I valued Allan not only as a coach, however, but, above all, as one of my greatest friends, unassuming yet with an impish sense of fun. My dad and I would go home with him for tea after a Saturday run to be welcomed by Lizzie, his wife. I frequently visited them on a Sunday, too, and even during the week after meeting him at his work in the masons' workshop below Glasgow Central Station. These visits to his home were especially valuable when I suffered injuries. He would massage me but, more importantly, inspire me with his canny advice. He was a great psychologist! Other club members would frequently drop in, especially on the Sunday, and Lizzie would busy herself providing meals for us all. I was proud to be one of her 'Scallywags' as she used to call us.

Margaret and I were delighted to have Lizzie and Allan as guests at our wedding in Stirling in 1960 and later they stayed with us on a weekend visit to our new home in Edinburgh. One of our last memories of them was walking along Portobello prom pushing Louise, our first child, in her pram. Allan suffered an unfortunate accident, being struck by a train as he was working on the line outside Central Station. Though cheerful as ever when I visited him in Glasgow Royal Infirmary, his health was poorly from then on and his untimely death was a great blow to me personally, to all Shettleston members and, as evidenced by the packed funeral Mass in St Bridget's Church, to athletes from all over the country.

Arthur Newton

Though I met him only twice, Arthur Newton, through the medium of his excellently written, privately published books and articles, influenced the theory and practice of my own running. He had revolutionised ultra-long distance in the 1930s after taking up running in his 40s for health reasons and giving up his farming in Southern Africa. He was a tall, very gentle, unassuming man who could, nevertheless, argue his case very forcibly in his writing. He gave a great deal of thought to, and personal experiment on, developing his ideas on all aspects of running, diet and general health. The title of one of his most influential books, *Commonsense Athletics*, perfectly epitomises his approach. Another most interesting book, *Races and Training*, contains excellent descriptions of his ultra-long and sometimes exotic feats of endurance in Africa, North America and Britain. He was a fascinating narrator and, after meeting him, I wrote an article in the Scots monthly, the *Mercat Cross*, which I entitled 'The Man Who Ran Against Horses' (and, incidentally, beat them!).

The first time I spoke to him was one Monday evening early in my road-running career at a meeting arranged by Walter J. Ross, the editor and publisher of the *Scots Athlete*, in Partick Burgh Halls, Glasgow. Unfortunately for Walter, only half a dozen turned up, but, fortunately for me, it did give me an opportunity for informal conversation and I was able to ask Arthur many questions about his life and ideas. I had a much longer and more directly personal talk with him one evening after my return from Vancouver when I was kindly invited to the home of Dr Clark, a friend of Arthur's, in Polmont.

The way he persisted with his running through injuries, illnesses and disappointments was a revelation to me. Odd little details from his writing stick in my mind, such as his common-sense approach to diet to suit the individual's needs, his trick of getting a rhythm or a tune in his head as he ran along – (he suggested, not too seriously perhaps, waltz time to avoid the constant stress on the same leg!) – and the need to occupy one's mind on a long run. This last point was most important for me. If, for example, as I started my run in Edinburgh, I were to think of arriving in Falkirk, the sheer distance would have seemed so overwhelming that I would never have lasted the first miles. I used to combat the problem in two ways: firstly by psychologically breaking down the distance, and secondly, by deliberately daydreaming (often imagining myself winning major championships!). I expand this further, later in the book, in Chapter Per Adua Ad?.

Arthur's most important influence on me, however, was his stressing the value of the long build-up in training with the emphasis on putting in the miles at a speed slower than racing speed. This agreed with my own view – in particular the avoidance of constant speed trials. Arthur's analogy of putting money in the bank and then continually drawing it out to see if it were still there I thought most apt. I know that I found myself running very much faster in shorter races when I had concentrated solely on training for the marathon and, indeed, I set new records in races

1953 Race Highlights

1953: The D. McNab Robertson Memorial Trophy

Record-breaking run North Berwick to GPO – 23 miles 2h 5mins 19sec (almost 33mins off previous record)

1954 Race Highlights the same year as the British Empire Games Marathon

The D. McNab Robertson Memorial Trophy; Hon. Life Member SMC for Empire Games Marathon win (Aug). The Coronation Cup (The Scottish Athlete of the Year) 1954; SAAA Championships 1954 Marathon 1st – Record Breaking run – 2h 35mins 22sec Extract from personal running diary

1955 Race Highlights

S.M.C. Championship 1955 1st S.A.A.A. Championships 1955 Marathon 1st – New Record 2hrs 25mins 50sec; The Crabbie Trophy; The D. McNab Robertson Memorial Trophy

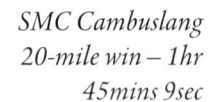

1955 Race Highlights

*SMC Cambuslang
20-mile win – 1hr
45mins 9sec*

1956 Race Highlights

June 1956 – Falkirk to Edinburgh Marathon – third consecutive year win 2hrs 33mins 36sec. The D. McNab Robertson Memorial Trophy; S.A.A.A. Championship Marathon 1st Trophy. Photo: Graham Everett and Allan Scally

1954 British Empire Games Vancouver Marathon

Original running strip and plimsoles worn for race, no. 697 with map of the Games in the background

1954 British Empire Games Vancouver Marathon

Scottish Team 1954 Blazer with gold medal in box and accompanying commemorative medal above.

From left: Programme of Entertainment for Competitors; Book of instructions for competitors; Garden Party Invitation 9 August 1954; Empire Stadium Official Programme for Track and Field; British Empire Games sticker; Transit Pass; Farewell Party Invitation; Special Dinner Invitation with Royal Highness Duke of Edinburgh; Identity Pass 697

1954 British Empire Games. Vancouver Marathon

7 August: First lap in the Empire Stadium, Vancouver

Seven miles in McGhee 697, Cox 335 and Peters 349

1954 British Empire Games. Vancouver Marathon

England's Jim Peters on verge of collapse

Half a lap to go

1954 British Empire Games. Vancouver Marathon

Nearing the finishing line and running through the tape

1954 British Empire Games. Vancouver Marathon

After the race with Willie Carmichael and Dr Euan Douglas

On the Rostrum – Helping Barnard

1954 British Empire Games. Vancouver Marathon

Gold Medal

1954 British Empire Games. Vancouver Marathon

Original wood block photo negative printing plate and glass negatives of the marathon

1954 After the Empire Games – Highlights

Celebrations at Windsor Road

Dad – Willie McGhee holding medal

1954 After the Empire Games – Highlights

Congratulated by Dunky Wright, 1930 Gold Medal Marathon Winner

Map of Empire Marathon Race Route

1996 Reunion

1996 Reunion with Jim Peters at the Flora London Marathon

such as the Nigel Barge Five Miles and the six miles stage in the Edinburgh to Glasgow Relay, where in earlier seasons when I was specifically training for such races my performances had been pretty mediocre.

These long easy runs emphasising mileage covered rather than speed are essential to give a background of fitness. It was Joe Walker who at the very beginning had convinced me of the value of such a preparation when he told me to relax and go out to enjoy the scenery and get a tan. Only once such a background is there (I am talking in terms not just of a few 100 miles but of some 1,000), did I find that speed training could be beneficial. I knew promising young contemporaries of mine who would start off by copying Gordon Pirie's schedule, for example, and, after achieving great times in training sessions, would fail on the big occasion such as the national championships.

I was introduced the hard way to speed or a type of modified Fartlek training when, under the guidance of Allan Scally, I trained with Eddie Bannon, the Scottish cross-country champion. Eventually I developed his eye for the country and could guess exactly where his bursts would begin, and, in the end, I was able to hold him and even continue the burst when he began to ease off. The real answer to improvement of first-class performance, of course, would have been a judicious blend of both steady easy running and speed training, but the easy build-up amassing mileage had to come first and was the real secret of success for me. Quite simply, I was determined to run more miles in the time I could afford to devote to training than any one of my rivals. No matter how slow these runs were, they were all recorded in my training notebooks or, in the words of Arthur Newton's analogy, deposited 'in the bank', and these increasing totals gave me not only a physical but also a psychological boost.

Willie McGhee

The fifth but by no means the least influential person in my development as a runner was, of course, my dad. He was never an athlete himself, being prevented by the harsh circumstances of his working life and the consequent ravages of ill health. He was born in Falkirk in 1901, seventh in a family of nine, and was brought up by an indomitable North East English mother after his father died. She eked out a meagre living by selling china to her neighbours, and my dad had to start work in the pits the day he reached his 14th birthday. The effects of coal dust were bad enough, but after six years he changed over to an environment even more harmful to his lungs – work as a process worker in Grangemouth in the Scottish Dyes, later taken over by ICI. In those days, he had to do things as part of his job, which later he would have been sacked on the spot for. Explosions were frequent, sometimes whole sheds going up, and he was in more than one of these incidents. When he married my mum, Jean Callaghan, in 1928, they set up home in a tiny two-roomed house in Graham's Road, Falkirk, about three miles away from the chemical plant. One of my earliest memories was the sound of the emergency services rushing to the scene of one of the explosions after which he lay blind for three weeks in hospital. More deadly, however, were the effects on his lungs, which eventually forced him to retire early and from which he died at the age of 66.

He would tell many humorous anecdotes about how he wasted time at school, volunteering, for example, when the inspectors were coming, to leave the classroom to get flowers for his teacher, which he somehow acquired from the local dump. One day he suffered for his enterprise, however, putting himself forward when the class was asked who the poor boys were. He was dispatched to the local draper who got rid of his unwanted stock by sending him home in full Highland dress! My English grandmother, staunchly independent and against accepting charity, was affronted and promptly marched him back to the shop. Despite his joking, he seriously regretted his lack of what he considered to be a proper education and he was determined to sacrifice everything so that his family of three would get the opportunities he had missed.

On a pitiful pre-war labouring rate, he would cycle straight from work without a proper meal and put in an evening doing the heavy work in the gardens of the various staff chemists for the princely sum of two shillings or two shillings and sixpence (10p or 12½p today). Later, I was glad to see him getting a part-time steward's job in the factory's recreation club. A teetotaller himself, he was nevertheless a very popular barman. He was then offered the full-time post as club steward, but we were very sorry for his health's sake when he had to refuse the offer as the tied, two-bedroomed house was too small for our family.

In spite of his material disadvantages, however, he was a born organiser in many different spheres. Even before he married, he ran the church young men's football team and all the activities of the 'White Heather Club', MC-ing all their dances and other social functions. Though often desperately short of money and frequently in ill health himself, he was the most charitable of men, giving of his time and energies to visit the sick and elderly. He always went to every bed in the hospital ward he would be visiting, leaving some small gift at each even if it were only a box of matches. He helped run the soup kitchens during the 1926 General Strike and was a leading member of the SVDP, a church society to help the poor. I remember, indeed, one beggar coming to our door and asking to speak to Mr St Vincent De Paul! A member of the first aid and rescue post during the war, he helped frequently with first aid courses and, later, he set up the Welcome Home Committee organising the gifts and subsequent events for the returning ex-service men in our area. Involved, too, in the founding of Camelon's Mariners' Day, he extended his organising activities over a much wider area, this time bringing in sports and athletics. Then, when we moved to a new housing area in a different part of the town, he began the Windsor Road Gala Committee and organised functions not only for the children but the elderly residents as well.

Though obviously a skilled and enterprising organiser who, given more propitious circumstances, might have risen far in business or politics, he was held back by an irrational fear that, because of his early education, he was a bad speller and therefore could not write. Of course, this was an absurd belief. He had no problems in speaking lucidly in public, but frequently he would ask me to vet his letters. Though I was an honours graduate in English with postgraduate qualifications in linguistics, I was never able to fault his expression or the construction of his sentences. All he really needed was a modern spell-checker! His lengthy, very frequent and inspiring letters to me when I was in the RAF were a model in fluency.

He was broad-minded politically and would support and give practical assistance to candidates depending on their individual qualities rather than their party labels. He tried to broaden my education by taking me along with him to union and political meetings of all persuasions. Not only did he do everything in his power to advance my education generally, however, but he became completely supportive, too, of all my tentative efforts in athletics, a sphere in which he had had no experience himself. I remember sending him a telegram to Gleneagles Hotel where he was on an industrial rehabilitation course for a back injury in 1946 and desperate to know how I had fared in my first attempt at the school mile. 'First. Broke record. Joe' was my succinct message.

From then on till the end of that brief summer season, he started to go with me to local track events but he was unable to do so during my five years of university competition throughout Britain and Ireland. It was when I began to compete in the road races at the various Highland Games after I had graduated, however, that he really began to accompany me regularly and I was greatly heartened by his support. Later, when I joined Shettleston Harriers, he became almost an honorary member and official himself, attending their Saturday training sessions and all their cross-country races and becoming a firm friend of Allan and Lizzie Scally. Indeed, he soon was a familiar figure to many runners, supporters and officials of other clubs. I remember, how, in one of the Edinburgh to Glasgow road relays, he even enlisted the help of Andy Forbes, the leading internationalist of one of our biggest rivals, Victoria Park, to drive him and Allan in my car as I ran my own stage. When I was out on the road, I would give him my valuables to keep for me. During one race in West Lothian, however, he unfortunately lost my gold presentation Parker pen. He was absolutely devastated and I was even more so at seeing him so upset.

One of his greatest thrills, however, was to ride in the RAF vehicle accompanying me all the way on my record-breaking run from North Berwick to Edinburgh on 8 December 1953, which I describe in detail in the chapter outlining my efforts to be chosen for the Empire and Commonwealth Games. From then on, he seized every opportunity to get out on the road during my actual races. Despite his worsening health problems, too, he even went with Shettleston Harriers on overnight trips when, calling ourselves Lanarkshire, we competed at Fort William in 1954 and Elgin in 1955. On the latter, as I mentioned earlier, he was astonished to find a bottle of whisky in his bed on the Saturday night – a gift arranged by Mrs Blandford, the energetic Games organiser and the local distillery owner – and he was a lifelong teetotaller! The following year, he managed to accompany Allan Scally and me on my ill-fated trip to the British Championships in Birkenhead.

I came to rely more and more on his advice and on our system of timekeeping, especially in the championship marathons when he would give me vital information about the competitors behind me. In these events, he depended on lifts in friends' cars or on the bus accompanying the race. So comforting did his presence become for me that on the day in 1955 when I shattered the Scottish marathon record by almost ten minutes, I nearly caused him to miss my finish on the track. As he passed me on the last mile up the hill from Leith to Meadowbank, after he had done our usual time-check on the gap between me and the next competitor, he shouted that they were now going straight ahead to the stadium. Though I was now so far in front that I could probably have been able to slow to a walk and still won comfortably (and I was running very strongly indeed), I yelled back, 'Not yet! Stay in sight!'

He obviously could not accompany me on my long training runs. We did manage, however, a lift for him from the father of Bob Sinclair, a Falkirk Victoria Harrier, on the Sunday before the above-mentioned championship. Bob ran with me for the first 20 miles from Falkirk and I then continued running easily over the last six miles to

Meadowbank to record a very respectable 2hrs 40mins for a training spin. We were delighted when Bob achieved his standard medal the following Saturday.

On another occasion, my dad even persuaded Louise, my sister, to accompany him on cycles when I set out on a full 26-mile run round Stirlingshire. They would cycle slowly ahead for a few miles, then wait and give me my time as I caught up. As the miles passed by, however, it became clear that it was the intrepid cyclists who were beginning to tire badly, and I ran away on the last mile to arrive home quite a bit ahead of them. They never sought to repeat the experiment!

One of my problems (which I discuss in a later chapter) was finding out the exact nature of the course in races. When a 14-mile road race, for example, was run from the first sports meeting to be organised in Callendar Estate in Falkirk, the route took us around minor roads unfamiliar to me in West Lothian. Dad, ever resourceful, solved my problem by getting a young workmate of his, who visited him when he was ill, to run me round the course the evening before the race on his motorcycle. I felt rather precarious on the back of the very powerful machine – I was never a good pillion passenger! – and I don't really know if I took in all that much as I hung on grimly.

In later years, when he was clearly unwell, nevertheless, he would still be anxious to go along to races, and, in spite of the fact that, at the end of one of the Edinburgh to Glasgow road relays, he turned very sick at the presentation ceremony in a Glasgow restaurant, I hadn't the heart to refuse his help. I cannot stress how invaluable his encouragement was right to the end of my active competing.

Typical of the man was one of his last public activities in 1964, four years before he died, when he organised and compered a reception for Bobby McGregor, Falkirk's world-famous freestyle swimmer – typical, too, that the audience that night was the old folks of the area, whose cause was so dear to his heart.

Chapter 12

Getting Lost

ONE OF my greatest fears in cross-country races especially, but in road races too, was simply not knowing where to go. It was most frustrating to build up a lead and then to find it being frittered away by having to wait for the next runner or, worse still, going off in the wrong direction. Of course, in theory, such a difficulty should never arise in properly organised competitions. Every junction should have been properly signposted or, better still, stewarded by experienced human markers. The old idea of laying a paper trail or, even sometimes today, scattering dabs of flour – both methods at the mercy of wind, rain or snow – is a recipe for disaster.

St Andrews
My first major experience of this problem occurred in my first year at university in the winter of 1946 during the annual six-mile cross-country race at St Andrews between teams from Glasgow and St Andrews universities. The leading runner for St Andrews, their half-mile track champion, set off at a blistering pace and broke completely from the field. I managed to keep relatively close behind him until we entered a narrow twisting path running

alongside a stream on our left. Turning one corner, however, I found that he had already disappeared round the one ahead. Just after that corner, beside a narrow wooden footbridge, stood a girl wearing a red undergraduate student gown. The course, most unusually for this period, was being marked by girl students. She smiled at me and mouthed something politely. I could not make out a word and simply kept running past her along the path.

Then, after covering some distance, I began to realise that something was wrong: I could see no one ahead and could hear no one behind. I decided that I had better double back. Before I reached the girl, however, I saw through the trees a string of competitors running on the other side of the stream. It looked no wider than the Bannock Burn, which I had often forded at school, so I at once plunged down into the water – and went under! I had to swim the few yards to the other bank. Clambering out and shivering in the windy chill of the dull winter's day, I found myself in the middle of a long trail of runners heading for a grassy hill, Scoonie Hill, which seemed to me then as steep as a coal bing! I managed to fight my way up the hill past the four or five runners ahead of me into what I eventually found was second place. The leader by now had completely disappeared. As I entered the town once more, I was heartily glad to see a red-clad girl student waving her arms. Again, I had no idea what she was saying, but I had been told to look for the blonde marking the last corner before the finish and this obviously was the girl.

A couple of seasons later when we had to travel for this fixture again, the St Andrews team held the race on their Dundee campus. This time, I was ready for their champion's tearaway tactics and I managed to hang on grimly a yard or so behind him throughout the race until the tape came into sight. Then I suddenly saw his shoulders twitch as he speeded up and I realised that he was feeling sick. Heartened by this sign of his distress, I managed to pull out a sprint finish past him. He never beat me again. I had learned a very important lesson, which was to stand me in good stead in the years to come: no matter how bad I was feeling towards the end of a race, my opponents were probably feeling worse and I determined to give no one any encouragement by showing signs of my own distress.

Linlithgow

In the early summer of 1947, at the end of my first university year, I won my first open race – the inaugural 'Round the Loch' race at the Linlithgow sports meeting held on the Peel, a stretch of the roughly triangular-shaped grassland between the ancient palace and the loch.

At first glance, there seemed no possibility at all of losing the course in this race. As we lined up at the start, we could take in what seemed to me to be all of the three miles-plus of the circuit round the loch. The path along the opposite north side was clearly visible. We would be running round the loch, keeping the water on our left hand.

As we started round the track, I at once took the lead and found that I was being guided south up the hill past the palace and then down into the main street of the town, where I was directed east towards Edinburgh. I assumed that letting the townsfolk see us like this was intended as an advertisement for the sports on the lochside. At the next junction, we were again steered left, down the road to Blackness, back in the general direction of the loch.

I could not see any official car or cycles ahead of us and I had no idea of how far we were to continue on this road or, indeed, of where we should go next. Glimpsing the water again at the end of a short alleyway on my left, I at once turned down the lane and, climbing over a gate, ran over a strip of grass straight for the water's edge. There was no path at all at this point as I swung right towards the end of the loch, so I simply ran as close to the water as I could, heading round the south-east corner of the loch. Fortunately, the next runner, Davie Clelland, our top senior and club captain at St Modan's AAC, had followed me and the rest of the field had followed him.

Then I came up against a complete impasse: the ground rose steeply at this point on the eastern end of the loch and a wooden barrier rose up from the water shoring up the bank. Some yards beyond, I could see a wooden swing gate and the path running back west along the north side of the loch. Obviously, this was the point at which we should have made contact with the loch again.

I dared not hesitate. Intent on taking the shortest route and completely forgetting my St Andrews experience, I plunged down straight into the water. Luckily, it was only knee-deep and the bottom proved to be fairly smooth as I ploughed past the barrier until I was able to scramble back on to the shore again and then on to the path. I still have no idea what the rest of the field did here. I presumed they were still on my heels and I simply hammered on as fast as I could along the smooth path to the west end of the loch, round the top and then back east to the sports meeting, where I finished an easy winner ahead of Davie Clelland, who had hung on to second place throughout.

I was proud to hand over to my mum my first open prize, an electric wall clock, which received pride of place in the kitchen of our new home in Windsor Road, into which we had moved only the previous evening.

RAF Cranwell

Though the rest of my races at university provided me with some crazy moments such as the 12ft wall I had somehow to get over when the Universities' International was held in Nottingham, it was not until I entered the RAF at the beginning of 1952 that the problem of getting lost in races really began in earnest. Three instances occurred during my spell of officer training at RAF Spitalgate near Grantham.

The Midlands Area RAF Cross-Country Championship was held at the RAF elite Cranwell College early in 1952. In the massed charge at the start from the playing fields, I followed my newly developed tactic of allowing myself to be carried along in the throng of bodies, avoiding as far as I could the flailing arms and legs around me. Then, after the first half-mile as the pace began to slacken, I began my own charge through the mob ahead and caught up with the leaders as we entered a long track leading through a belt of woodland. I learned afterwards that we were following the route of an old Roman road. Surprisingly quickly, I found my breathing settling and I decided to thrust myself into the lead and break from the leading pack. When we emerged into the sunlight again, however, and I saw fields stretching round us with no sign of stewards or flags, I realised that it had happened again! I hadn't a clue where to go next.

Having established a lead, I certainly was not going to wait for the pursuing runners. Over the fields to my right, I could see, above the trees, the famous Cranwell clock tower, which had been hit by an aircraft during the war, so I swung right and proceeded to make my own course roughly in a wide circle round the tower. Fortunately, all the other runners followed me.

It was supposed to be a seven-mile race but I must have made it nearer ten before I approached the playing fields again and saw the group of officials round the finish. Unfortunately, there were a couple of rugby matches in progress between me and the tape but I decided to take the shortest route in a direct line straight through them, ignoring the astonished looks of the players as I passed. After I finished, I looked round to see absolute chaos as hundreds of runners brought the rugby to a halt as they streamed across. As everyone had taken the same route throughout, the results were accepted and I was then set for the finals in London in March.

Nottingham – Army Depot

The officials were not so complaisant, however, at Nottingham on Wednesday, 6 February 1952. The date sticks in my mind as I was sitting in the back of an RAF truck at traffic lights in Leicester when someone shouted that the King (George VI) had just died. The RAF Spitalgate team were on their way to Nottingham to compete against an army team.

As, this time, there were only two teams of nine competing, the start was much less frantic and I soon found myself in the lead alongside the army champion. As we reached the top of a fairly steep field and passed through a gate in the hedge, I could see no sign of the stewards (army privates) who had left well ahead of us to take up their positions round the course. Turning to the army runner beside me, I asked, 'Where now?' He grunted back, 'Haven't a clue. I'm a stranger here.'

I decided not to hesitate and, seeing a road at the foot of the field ahead, made a beeline for it. I sensed the gap between us growing and I then turned left in what I hoped was the direction of the army depot. I kept running along the road as I was wearing rubber-studded cross-country shoes and managing quite comfortably on the hard surface, but I knew that my opponent was wearing spikes and would be finding the road decidedly awkward if we stuck to it.

Reaching the outskirts of the city, I found the streets quite busy with workers going home and I received some baffled looks as I kept inquiring, 'Where's the ordnance depot?' I don't know whether it was my Scots accent or my breathless gasps that caused the problem!

At last, turning a corner, I saw the group of officials round the finish. They handed me a metal disc and, to my amazement and disgust, I saw the number '6' on it. The army champion then came hirpling in next, followed by the entire RAF team. I protested vehemently that I was first, not sixth, and adamantly refused to accept my disc. The first five apparently were army runners who had been so far behind that the markers had appeared in their correct positions before they reached them and then steered them on the planned course. It later transpired that these tardy stewards had been sitting behind a hedge having a smoke!

I had caused such a fuss, however, that the race was declared null and void and the offending markers, no doubt, found themselves facing a charge.

RAF Spitalgate

The following comedy of errors occurred within the next two or three weeks at my home station, RAF Spitalgate, and did not directly affect me, though I suppose I was indirectly one of the causes.

The Inter-course Cross-Country Championship was run on the afternoon of the day when I was acting course commander for Blue Course. My duties were simple: I had to give the orders for the day and march the officer cadets from one class or activity to the next. Addressing the flight on morning parade, however, I told them on my own initiative that everyone had to turn out for Blue Course in the afternoon's race. As the five other courses put forward teams with a maximum of nine runners each, our course's

60-odd competitors certainly swelled the numbers who lined up for the start.

The course was simple, starting off on the rough grass round the perimeter of the grass airfield, navigating past the obstacles of the assault course on the right and top sides of the airfield, then diverging into the country for a short loop before returning back down the left side of the airfield and along the foot to the finish. There really was no possibility of getting lost. I knew the course well, having trained over it regularly, and, even for the complete novices on my own course, the only part that required any marking was the short loop into the country.

I took the lead at once and won easily, not realising till afterwards what had been going on behind me. When the leading group behind me were running round the top of the airfield, most of my course were still toiling up the right-hand side and a few at the rear had already started walking and even trying to snatch fly puffs at a cigarette! Then, in the absence of markers on this part of the course, some had the bright idea of cutting across the top corner of the airfield to reduce the gap. What they did not realise was that their antics were being observed from above by Flt Lt Murphy, the moustachioed air ace in charge of our course. He had gone up in a tiny Tiger Moth, the pre-war training biplane. Deciding to 'buzz' them, he swooped down only a few feet above their heads and, terrified out of their wits, they had to fling themselves flat on the grass.

The incident was the talk of the changing room afterwards and some of the cadets speculated about what action he would take later against the culprits. Privately, I thought that, having so thoroughly (and literally!) put the wind up them, he wouldn't take the matter any further for, though he was a strict disciplinarian, he had a good sense of humour, and my surmise proved to be correct.

The matter was not to end there, however, for some bright sparks saw the opportunity for what they imagined would be a great practical joke. Personally, I thought it rather cruel and did not support it. Picking on one of the most inoffensive of those involved, a little, mild-mannered, rather diffident but likeable cadet from Liverpool, Len Smith (a pseudonym!), they proceeded to 'wind him up'. Didn't he realise how serious was his crime, running across the path of an incoming aircraft and forcing it to take evasive action? As Len grew more and more worried, they assured him that it was a court martial offence and one that would almost certainly mean the 'chop' from the course.

The joke then took a much more dramatic turn when the door was peremptorily thrust open and a flying officer followed by two pilot officers marched in. He announced that he was from Airfield Safety and Security and demanded to see Officer Cadet Len Smith. In reality, he was one of the older cadets from one of the senior courses who, like me, had been commissioned before his course began and thus possessed full 'best blue' officer's uniform. He inveighed against the so-called crime with dire threats of court martial, but then appeared to relent somewhat and offer a possible way out of his predicament for Len. If Len would write a formal official letter of confession and apology, he would see it handed over to the Air Officer Commanding Safety and Security, Group Captain Mango Chutney. Len was so anxious to comply that the absurd name did not register with him and he hastened to write the letter on the paper so conveniently supplied by the bogus security officer. It began with the official rubric 'Sir, I have the honour to confess ...' They put it in an envelope and marched out again.

Then, even more cruelly, the letter was later published in the course magazine. However, Len had the last laugh.

He took the joke and ridicule in such good part that his popularity soared and I am convinced it played quite a significant part in his securing his pass and subsequent commission.

RAF Dishforth

The following year, 1953, saw me well established as education officer at RAF Turnhouse, Edinburgh, and consequently in a different area – the Northern Area – for the RAF Cross-Country Championship. The race was held at RAF Dishforth near Ripon in Yorkshire. The same confusion was to occur, however, as in the previous year's Midland Championship at Cranwell.

As before, I fought my way through the massed field at the end of the first half-mile and caught up with the leader, Corporal Pat Ranger, the RAF champion and English internationalist, who was to finish third in the International Cross-Country Championship.

Running together, the two of us broke from the others and, passing through a gate without noticing any markers, continued straight on up a long field. The rest of the competitors behind us, however, were directed to the left at a right angle to us, along the foot of the field. We had almost reached the top end before we became aware of frantic shouting and, glancing round, saw the long stream of runners heading rapidly away from us. At once we cut diagonally back across the field towards the front bunch, Ranger setting a furious pace and I hanging grimly on behind him. We must have been in the late 20s when we finally made contact. I would have been quite happy then to tuck in and get my breath back but Ranger made an even more exacting spurt and, gasping, I somehow managed to dredge up the energy to follow on his heels. It was then that I really appreciated the value of a pacemaker as he took me past man after man until we were once more in the lead. Even then, however, he did not slacken his speed, determined to make a clean break from the pursuing group, and somehow or other I was able to keep in reasonable contact with him until we finished comfortably first and second.

I was to turn the tables on Ranger in the following year's championship, held again at Dishforth in very different snowbound conditions, but that story I have already told in an earlier chapter.

Lanarkshire Cross-Country Championship

A similar mishap occurred to me a year or so later in the Lanarkshire Cross-Country Championship and cost me the chance of one of my rare cross-country victories over Eddie Bannon, the Scottish cross-country champion.

Bannon was the outstanding cross-country personality of the 1950s. His early promise in finishing fourth as a junior in the Senior International Championship in Paris was to see him develop into one of Scotland's finest-ever cross-country runners and captain of the national team. He had a natural grace and balance that enabled him to skim over the roughest country. In cross-country championships, I usually saw his back all the time, only once beating him in the National Championship in 1955 on Hamilton racecourse when I finished third. I did have the edge over Eddie on the road, however, my marathon training sharpening me up remarkably over much shorter road distances (for example, my wins in the Nigel Barge Five Miles road race in 1955 and 1956, on the latter occasion setting a new record of 22mins 40secs). He was also a fine track runner, but in my only track race against him, the six miles at Barrachnie in December 1955, I managed to beat him in 30mins 31secs.

The weather on the day of the Lanarkshire Cross-Country Championship in question was absolutely vile. Not only had it been raining steadily for what seemed like days on end, creating very muddy and slippery conditions even on the grassy parts of the course and making the naturally heavy parts over the ploughland much more sticky, but that day a raw chill wind had risen that sapped our strength even more insidiously. The conditions, indeed, were so bad that even Bannon was struggling, especially on the latter half of the course.

For once, I was able to stay with him fairly comfortably. I took the lead and actually broke free from him with less than two miles of the seven to go. The big snag today, however, was the use of paper to mark the trail – the first time I had ever encountered this method of marking in a major championship.

As I ploughed through the mud at a gate between two fields, with the wind blowing from the right against my face, the inevitable occurred. I could see at first no trace of scattered paper. Then I glanced uphill to my left and glimpsed something white on the hedge near the top of the field. I promptly turned left, shortening my stride as I battled up the hill. I had covered about 100 yards when I heard a shout from behind me. Eddie had passed the gate and was running at a right angle to me at the foot of the hill. He gave a brief wave, pointing in the direction in which he was running and continued straight ahead. Obviously, the wind had played havoc with the paper! I had to try to cut across the field back on to the intended trail, but then found myself floundering along and facing quite a considerable gap behind Eddie with too short a distance to go. I eventually finished second about 50 yards behind him.

The decision by the race organisers to lay a paper trail on such a windy day had been an absolutely disastrous one!

Even when I was at Glasgow University, where the cross-country team was called the 'Hares and Hounds', we had never resorted to such a method for marking races.

Callendar Estate, Falkirk

While getting lost was not an infrequent occurrence when running cross-country, it was certainly much rarer in road races as there was almost always a pilot car ahead of us. Training on the road was a very different matter, of course, as I deliberately sought out the little-used lanes and minor roads in order to relax and avoid passing too many people. Indeed, much of the pleasure of training was to find unexpected tracks over stretches such as the moors round Slamannan or the hills between Stirling and Denny.

Though, with the presence of official cars, we couldn't really get lost in road races, I still liked to familiarise myself as much as possible, however, with the routes of the races for tactical purposes, such as determining the best places to put in a spurt, for example. Where I wasn't able to get over the whole distance beforehand, I tried as far as I could to jog over the last half-mile or so if we were returning to the same point we started from, as in most Highland Games.

This policy paid off for me on one notable occasion in the summer of 1955 when the race was a 14-mile one starting and finishing at the town council sports meeting in Callendar Estate, Falkirk. The race started and finished with a lap of the track laid out in front of Callendar House and took us up through the surrounding woods and out of a minor estate gate on to the back road between Glen Village and Laurieston, where the official car was waiting to pilot us along the B roads through Redding, Rumford and Brightons to Linlithgow Bridge and then back to the same rear entrance to the estate behind Laurieston. I had been taken over the public roads on the course on the Friday evening by a young workmate of my dad on the back of his motorcycle. Nevertheless, I arrived early the next afternoon before the race and still jogged over the half-mile to three-quarters of a mile of woodland track to the estate gate and then back to the sports meeting. It was only then that I realised how different the track looked from the opposite direction and I noted at least one point of possible confusion where another track intersected ours.

I raced into the front right from the gun and then put in a spurt when we reached the road outside the estate. Running alone, I had a comfortable race when I realised that I had established a fair lead over the chasing group and I was able to pull out a grandstand finish for the benefit of the waiting crowds. When I had a good lead in such races, it was a favourite ploy of mine to save a little back for my entry into the stadium. Indeed, I could remember the commentator broadcasting to the crowd as I won the 13 miles race at Dundee North End Games earlier that season, 'He left the track like a half-miler and here he comes back like a quarter-miler!'

As I completed my lap of the track to the tape and looked back, however, I was rather surprised to see that no other competitors had yet come in sight from the gap in the trees. In fact, it must have been almost ten minutes before the next runner finished. It was my friend, Bob Sinclair from Falkirk Victoria Harriers, who was followed by a string of runners. He was over the moon with his second place but was completely mystified as he had thought that he was running fourth when he had entered the estate again. The two more fancied runners ahead of Bob had obviously taken the wrong turning at the fork in the wood and lost out to him before being diverted back into the race again.

Chapter 13

Danger to Life and Limb

I DESCRIBED in earlier chapters some of the dangers I encountered in cross-country races such as having to swim at St Andrews, falling into a burn in one of the Lanarkshire cross-country championships, being attacked and hurled down a ploughed slope in the RAF Championship and falling over a fence and ripping my back on the barbed wire in the Midland Championship. Road races, of course, could be even more perilous because of the other traffic on the public roads. One of the competitors behind me in the Perth to Dundee race, for example, was knocked down by a car at the Ninewells junction near Dundee. Luckily, his injuries were not too serious but that was the end of the race for him.

In the London to Brighton Relay, too, the sheer volume of very slow-moving traffic meant that we were running in a constant and hazardous pall of car fumes as well as having to swerve and break step to avoid suddenly braking vehicles. Indeed, on one of the roundabouts beyond Croydon Airport, a car cut in front of Peter Pirie and me. I still don't know how its window was not shattered as Pirie hammered on the glass with his metal relay baton to fend it off.

Some of the most dangerous moments that I experienced when I was running, however, did not happen in actual races. (For example, the various incidents when I was attacked by dogs during my training runs described in a later chapter and as mentioned previously nearly drowning the Shettleston Harrier, John Eadie.) One of the most hair-raising events was the run through Glasgow city centre by 'the Knights of the Fiery Cans'. This was a stunt designed to gain publicity for the forthcoming Students' Charities Day.

It was a dull Saturday morning in the winter of 1948 when three lines of Glasgow University Hares and Hounds jogged up and down, shivering in the cold breeze outside the City Chambers in George Square. Our outlandish appearance – bare arms and legs protruding from silver-painted cardboard armour – was already attracting a crowd of onlookers. Each of us clutched a makeshift torch – an open can stuffed with oily rags and screwed on to a short wooden pole. I don't know whose was the original idea but our whole get-up was no doubt organised by our indefatigable secretary and captain, Graham Jardine.

The first sign of trouble occurred when the Lord Provost tried to ignite the first of the torches. For a moment or two, nothing happened and then, suddenly, the flame leapt up with a 'whoosh' that had him jumping smartly back. The crowd cheered, hoping for more excitement. We managed, however, to light all of our torches without mishap and, to another burst of cheering, we turned and ran more or less smartly three-abreast round the square past Queen Street Station and then up Buchanan Street. We occupied much of the left carriageway as I at least (like most of my fellow-runners!) was holding my torch out at arm's length, wide of my body, not knowing how flammable was the silver paint on my armour and having no desire to perform a desperate striptease before the crowds! The streets were now very busy and we must have caused quite an obstruction as we passed perilously close to the line of tramcars in the centre of the road with passengers cheering (or catcalling?) from the windows.

It was when we turned left into Sauchiehall Street that things really began to get very scary. The breeze must have grown stronger and the torches seemed to flare up even more fiercely. Suddenly some of the burning rags fell from the can of the runner in front of me and I found myself desperately trying to hurdle the flaming mess without spilling the contents of my own can. Other runners must have been experiencing similar difficulties to judge from the yells around me.

Somehow or other, we reached Charing Cross and crossed to the comparative quiet of the western part of Sauchiehall Street and then into Kelvin Way without injuring ourselves or the passers-by. I was never so glad to reach our journey's end safely at the university gates, where the cans were doused. I suppose that it was regarded as a successful advertising stunt but it was certainly one that might easily have resulted in the very worst kind of publicity!

A much happier and far more prestigious event was the Fifth Centenary Glasgow University Torch run on 5 and 6 January 1951, but it too was not without some considerable hazards. A relay team of 12 runners carried the symbolic torch of learning from the tiny Roxburghshire hamlet of Bedrule, the birthplace of our founder, Bishop William Turnbull, through the Borders to Glasgow. On this occasion, instead of our usual black, we were superbly kitted out in white polo-necked sweaters and singlets, embroidered with the university badge, and white satiny shorts edged in black and gold.

A host of academic and civic dignitaries, resplendent in their colourful robes and headed by Colonel Walter Elliot, our previous rector, and Mr John MacCormick, our present one, packed the little hilltop kirk for an impressive dawn service. Sitting near the front, I felt rather incongruously dressed with my graduate gown and hood on top of my running kit as I was due to run the second leg of the relay. Then, after a fanfare from four trumpeters of the Ninth Lancers, Colonel Elliot lit the two-foot-long, pitch-covered brand from a blazing log fire outside the kirk and, to the skirl of the pipes and drums of the University Training Corps, John Jardine, that year's Hares and Hounds captain, was sent on his way. John was the only one who had to risk carrying the flaring torch on his three-mile first lap to Menslaws where I was waiting for him and exchanged the torch for an 18-inch flameproof brass lantern designed by the University Engineering Department.

Safe from burning, I thought, as I ran off briskly, but not from skidding on the snow and ice-covered Border roads! Overhead, thankfully, the weather conditions were fair enough but the cold was intense and, foolishly, I had elected to doff my sweater before I began. I therefore increased my pace and thus, half-skating, I managed to keep my balance more or less successfully to the end of my three-mile stint. I really must have looked chilled, however, as I handed over the lantern for I was offered a hot bath at a nearby farmhouse and afterwards found that the farmer's wife had prepared a plate of ham and eggs for me!

Other members of the team were not so fortunate. Conditions underfoot became even more treacherous later, especially round Abbotsford, and Roddy Paterson fell and cut his knee but somehow or other managed to keep the torch upright and still lit. The drivers of the accompanying vehicles were also finding the going dangerous. Indeed, the Duke of Buccleuch's car on its way to the changeover point skidded into a lorry and he arrived too late at Newtown St

Boswells to hand the torch to Peter Endicott, who was to carry it to Melrose Abbey.

Conditions became particularly bad at St Ronan's Lodge near Innerleithen. Graham Jardine, on his last few 100 yards before handing over to his brother, John, signalled to our bus as we passed him that the torch had gone out. I grabbed the reserve lantern, which preserved the original flame, and ran back round the bend towards him before he should reach the crowd at the changeover. An enterprising photographer, however, followed me and took the picture that was repeatedly published in newspapers and magazines throughout the country and overseas under the caption, 'The Torch Changes Hands'. It showed Graham running in one direction and myself facing the other way trying to maintain my balance on the ice and wearing a student's red gown over my shorts and bare legs. Absurdly too, (letting the cat out of the bag!), each of us was clutching a torch.

Worse was to come at this changeover, however. Our pilot car and the bus with the runners and the band became stuck one behind the other on the narrow icy road. John by this time was already well on his way and the problem was to get me to the next rendezvous point for the last three-mile run into Peebles. Fortunately, *The Scotsman* reporter gave me a lift in his car so that I was waiting in time for John to arrive.

The press and magazine coverage was phenomenal, even including representatives from America, and their presence lent an element of farce to the proceedings at Peebles where we were to be welcomed to lunch. I had to come running up to the Old Kirk and hand the torch to Provost Daniels at least five or six times at the behest of the newsreel cameramen!

Later in the day and the further north and west we went, the underfoot conditions began to improve dramatically and, in the evening, all 12 of us, with Graham Jardine, a former captain, carrying the torch, made a spectacular entry into Lanark through the crowds to the floodlit Cross where we had been preceded by the band. The following afternoon, Provost Russell sent the torch on its way again to be welcomed at each stage by civic dignitaries in Hamilton, Cambuslang and Rutherglen.

This second day of the run was very different from the first. Yesterday's dangers of ice and snow-packed roads had entirely disappeared. Today's occasional mild drizzle gave us no problems at all. Now, however, the hazards would soon prove to be from the torches themselves.

As darkness fell, the 12 of us ran the last lap together through the city suburbs with David Johnstone, the University Athletic Club's President, and John Jardine constantly exhorting us to slow the pace in order to keep to the time schedule. We dared not arrive too early! We then stopped briefly in the carriageway at Glasgow Green for David to exchange the brass lantern for a naked torch again and we continued on to the Mercat Cross where Lord Provost Warren received the torch on behalf of the city. Here we all lit two-foot candle torches from David's and ran on past the Old College in the High Street to Cathedral Square to be welcomed by the minister and our rector and ex-rector. The platform was surrounded by a huge crowd of singing students, each of whom seemed to be carrying unlit candles similar to ours. We began passing on the flame to those nearest us before hurrying to the bus to change out of our running kit.

In no time at all, the square was blazing with light. Officially, 1,500 candles were supposed to have been issued but there were over 3,000 students in the crowd and everyone, it seemed to me, was clutching one. It took some time to marshal them into some semblance of order in lines four or five abreast before the procession moved off, led by three pipe bands – the City of Glasgow Police, the University Training Corps and the Red Hackle.

The traffic in the city centre – cars, buses and trams – had come to a complete standstill and the pavements were lined by crowds of spectators. I was glad that I was in the comparative safety of the more staid front line, keeping a safe distance from the torches on either side of me. Glancing back as we processed along Sauchiehall Street, I saw that the singing and chanting lines behind us had swelled out to more than a dozen wide, stretching right across the roadway as the marchers tried to keep clear of some of their more exuberant companions who were waving their torches about in time with the music. Some of the spectators, indeed, were backing off rather apprehensively from the flames but others more daring among them were even joining in and marching alongside, thus intensifying the congestion.

Again I was thankful to be ahead of the crush. I had problems enough with my own candle without having to dodge other people's! Hot grease was now dripping freely down the handle and I tried to protect my hand, my Blue's blazer and, most importantly, the academic gown borrowed from my old primary headmaster, John Farrell. The small cardboard disc above the handle was an adequate enough shield only if I remembered to hold the candle absolutely straight upright.

In the front line we faced another potential threat from the two motorcyclists who were wobbling slowly along ahead of the procession. They had acquired enthusiastic pillion passengers – two girls who were excitedly waving their torches. Luckily, however, the gap between us tended to increase as we turned into Kelvin Way up towards the University.

As we reached the gates, I risked another glance back downhill; the sight of the apparently endless river of moving lights was striking – 'a chain of fire' as one newspaper was to describe it. The most spectacular (and dangerous!) moment was still to come, however. Ahead of us, only the streetlamps broke the darkness as we came to a halt. Then David and next John hurled their torches on to the dark shape of the bonfire. As the rest of us in the team followed suit, the flames suddenly mushroomed up. At the same instant, the tower and the whole Gothic mass of the university buildings were dramatically floodlit and the huge beams of five powerful searchlights shot vertically upwards behind them.

We stood gazing up at the breathtaking transformation – but only for a moment, however, before the full danger of our present situation hit us. The shouting crowds from the procession behind us broke ranks and swarmed towards us with the one intention of hurling their own contributions on to the bonfire. Ducking below the hail of torches, we dodged back through the mob till we reached a safe distance from which to enjoy the pipe bands and the raucous singing that ensued.

Passing acquaintances and strangers alike were repeating to us the same comments that we had heard so many times over the past two days: we must be exhausted; what a tremendous feat it was to cover such a long distance (well over 100 miles). To us, of course, our three-mile stints were nothing. We could, indeed, have run much faster! It was the overcoming of such adverse weather and road conditions that gave us satisfaction. I felt sorry that my unforgettable and historic experiences were coming to an end, but, at the same time, I was exhilarated and glad, too, that I had come through them unscathed.

Chapter 14

The Perils of Speaking Engagements

FOR DECADES after the Vancouver race, even right up to the present one, I was still receiving invitations to speak to various societies and social clubs that often had little or no connection with athletics or sport generally. I resolutely refused, however, to become a handy, unpaid 'filler-in' of slots in the social calendar of such groups.

Nevertheless, remembering how I had some influence on future champion athletes like Tommy Malone and Mike Ryan, I made an exception with running clubs or schoolchildren, for example, speaking to the young members of Aberdeen Athletic Club and to Banchory Primary School children in the mid-1980s or being one of the main speakers at the Glasgow University Hares and Hounds 75th Anniversary Reunion in 1996 and at the Falkirk Victoria Harriers Centenary Dinner in 2001.

No matter how diverse had been these organisations and clubs to which I had been invited to speak in earlier years, I had been able to use basically the same fund of material – namely, my experiences running marathons – simply adapting certain anecdotes to suit the age, sex or background of the audience. Indeed, with those clubs that had absolutely no connection with sport, these stories about what it felt like to run a marathon were often even more effective in capturing and holding the interest of the listeners. As these were my own personal experiences that I was narrating, I needed no notes and, indeed, I soon found myself able to anticipate my audiences' reactions, manipulate my pauses and apparent hesitations and make my comments seem impromptu.

More dubiously, however, this material was not quite suitable for official campaigns promoting health, for example, and I became reluctant to become involved in such activities. I shall never forget being invited in the late 1950s to speak at an anti-tuberculosis campaign at a little mining village. I found myself teamed with a young doctor not much older than myself when we arrived at the local primary school. Accompanied by a local county councillor, we sat facing an almost empty classroom. The audience consisted of a couple of children at the front and three old ladies at the back. The old councillor had obviously done his homework for he began what was clearly going to be a fairly technical (and not very appropriate!) discourse – 'There are two types of tuberculosis – the bovine and the pulmonary.' Fortunately, he was interrupted by the arrival of one of the Miners' Welfare officials who informed us that we should not expect any more latecomers as 'this is the night that the pictures come to the village'. Our chairman, undaunted, then announced: 'If the mountain won't come to Mahomet, then Mahomet would just have to go to the mountain,' and we had to follow him out to the Miners' Welfare Hall.

We were ushered into a small room on the opposite side of a corridor from the main hall and sat listening to the general din. The noise from the projector showing Donald O'Connor and the Talking Mule was punctuated by various yells that rose to a crescendo at one point when the hall door opened and someone was ejected from the audience. The doctor and I were looking apprehensively at each other when our door opened and the Miners' Welfare chairman came in.

'Are youse yins a' doctors?' he asked, and then, interrupting my hurried disclaimer, astonished us by his next remarks. 'Weel then, I'd jist like to give you a few tips on speaking in public. When you go in, they'll a' shout at you. Dinnae worry. They dae it to me. Noo, who's gaun to speak first?'

Quickly realising that my only hope lay in the value of surprise, I seized the initiative and volunteered to precede the doctor.

At the end of one reel of the film, we were ushered on to a narrow strip of platform in front of the large screen. My throat was immediately caught by the fuggy atmosphere and my mouth seemed to dry up completely. I was appalled to see that at least 90 per cent of the audience consisted of children of all ages, from toddlers crawling about the front row, ostensibly in the care of their older siblings, to young teenagers at the back. They were clearly taken aback by the unusual sight of the group arriving on the platform and the din subsided to a relative silence.

Mercifully, the chairman, knowing his audience, introduced us exceedingly briefly and I plunged into my harangue. I haven't the faintest idea now what I said about the value of keeping fit but, sensing the low boredom threshold of my audience, I lasted for about a couple of minutes before hastily turning to introduce my fellow sufferer. The hall erupted into wild cheering and, ignoring protocol, I immediately escaped out into the corridor, leaving the doctor to his fate! I fancied that he looked rather shaken afterwards. I know that I certainly was and I mentally resolved: 'Never again!'

The annual Burns Supper was another type of function to which I was obviously being invited simply as a well-known name, but I was intrigued by the very different and traditional remit I was being offered. I decided to risk the challenge, though it certainly did involve me in rather a lot of detailed written preparation. I have spoken at only three Burns Suppers in my life, however, and I can state quite categorically that, Burns-lover as I am, there will never be another one for me!

Two of the invitations were for suppers on 25 January 1955 and 1956, and both were to give the Toast to the Lassies. The first was in Falkirk at the BBC Westerglen club and I spent some considerable time in preparing my notes. My theme, very briefly, was that the poets were universally in praise of the ladies – until they married them! – and Burns, I averred, was no exception. I supported my claim with lots of quotations from a wide range of English literature (a bad blunder at a Burns Supper!) though the Bard himself with such efforts as 'Epitaph on a Henpecked Husband' provided me with plenty of ammunition. These quotations I carefully typed in red in my notes so that they would stand out. Having derided the married ladies at some length, however, I then switched round and proceeded to demolish my own case by arguing that Burns, of course, had his tongue in his cheek all the time and I then went swiftly on to extol his praise of the fair sex before concluding with my Toast to the Lassies. My speech went down well with the guests, and a young lady, who had obviously had her reply well prepared in advance and was careful not to deviate from it, stood up and thanked me for all the nice things I had said about the lassies.

Emboldened by my success, I decided to use exactly the same material the following year in Glasgow at the Rutherford Kirk Ladies Burns Supper. It was a much larger affair and, from my place at the top table on the platform, I looked down on a crowded hall and was somewhat disconcerted to see that there were very few men present, the audience consisting mainly of ladies of quite a mature age – in fact, most of them reminded me of my granny! They listened in stony silence to my diatribe against the ladies but I comforted myself with the knowledge that my final demolition of my own case would be lavishing praise on them. Then disaster struck! As I turned the small pages of my notes, two of the pages stuck together and I found myself beginning my final invitation to the toast having omitted most of the praise! The matronly lady who stood up to reply to me gave me a grim smile and slowly intoned, 'Man was Made to Mourn.' She then began to lambast me. Clearly, she was able to think on her feet!

It was more than 20 years before I dared accept another invitation to speak at a Burns Supper, this time in Aberdeen. My name was still being brought up in the media references to the Vancouver Marathon, especially every four years when the Commonwealth Games came round or when some athlete collapsed in a race. This time I was tempted by the invitation because my remit was to be the Immortal Memory – the most important speech of the evening. Indeed, it was generally considered an honour to be asked to give this toast and tradition demanded that the speaker should be able to say something original about the poet.

Fortunately, I had recently been one of the first to be awarded the new Master of Letters Degree in Scottish Literature from Aberdeen University and one of my major dissertations had been on Burns and the French Revolution. Among other texts, I had researched Burns' letters and found some very interesting and not widely known material. I would be able to tell, for example, how he had bought carronades from Carron Iron Works, Falkirk, and tried to ship them to the French revolutionaries, or how, at a theatrical performance in Dumfries, he had instigated the singing of the revolutionary chant 'Ça Ira' instead of the national anthem as was customary. When the authorities investigated his behaviour, his abject denial of the charges, I argued, was a desperate attempt to retain his post as an excise officer in order to be able to support his wife and children. Leavened by a few jokes, including some humorous references to my previous experiences of Burns Suppers, this material, I was quietly confident, would provide a suitable theme for the main speech of the evening and I entitled it 'Burns, the Revolutionary'.

My first doubts began when I heard the preliminary wailing notes from the anteroom as the piper began to lead in the steaming haggis, carried by one of the waiters. It was then that I suddenly noticed a dagger on the table opposite my place. Whispering to the chairman for the evening, a lady on my right, I asked, 'What's this for?'

'Oh, for sticking into the haggis when you've finished reciting the poem to it,' she whispered in her turn.

'But I am giving the Immortal Memory,' I hissed back.

She looked at me blankly and replied, 'Yes, the Immortal Memory – to the Haggis.'

I nearly collapsed. What kind of Burns gathering was I supposed to be addressing? 'The Immortal Memory is to Burns himself!' I retorted, 'and that's what I've prepared.'

'Well, you'll just have to do both,' she answered. 'No one else at this table will know the poem.'

'But I know only the first few lines!' I gasped.

I knew many of Burns' works off by heart and could even have made a fair stab at the lengthy 'Tam O' Shanter', the other main work of the evening, but 'To a Haggis' had never been a favourite of mine.

'Even if you had only given me some warning to bring my copy of the poems, I could have read it all,' I groaned.

She hurriedly shook her head as the piper, having finished his procession round the room, stopped opposite me and the waiter deposited the platter containing the haggis on the table.

Rather shakily I rose to my feet. 'Fair fa' your honest sonsie face, Great chieftain o' the puddin'-race,' I began and somehow managed, fluently enough, through the first three lines before hurriedly impaling the haggis with the dirk. I immediately apologised for my brevity, making the excuse that, in the unfortunate absence of the reciter, I had had to take on a double duty at the last minute. Then before the gathering could recover, I plunged into the Immortal Memory.

I was by profession an experienced lecturer able to watch the faces of my listeners and, with a brief downward glance at times, adjust the tempo, emphasis and content of my notes to suit their reactions. I knew that my speech was going down well – indeed, very well – with some to judge by their rapt expressions, but there was a glazed look in the eyes of some of the others and a smirk on the faces of one couple especially that indicated that the drinks had already been flowing freely. Inwardly I was irritated by the attitude of the latter and that made me determined to catch and hold their attention. I therefore became even more energetic in my tone and emphasis before concluding with a rousing peroration – a mock-Burnsian stanza that I had written myself, inviting them all to stand up and toast the Bard.

My speech had undoubtedly made a successful impact especially with the genuine lovers of Burns who were profuse with their congratulations. Indeed, one of them, a local dentist, hurried over as soon as the tables were being cleared in preparation for the dance afterwards and was fulsome in his praise and his inquiries for further information. Even one of the glassy-eyed guests whom I had suspected of lack of interest hailed me with the congratulation, 'Man, you'd have made a grand trade union leader!' Nevertheless, my mind was already made up. 'This was the last time!' I resolved to myself. For me, too many of the frequenters of these gatherings are interested not in paying tribute to the poet but simply in grasping the opportunity for an annual 'booze-up'.

Chapter 15

Then and Now

THERE ARE many striking differences between the world of athletics in general (and marathon running in particular) as it was 50 years ago and as we know it today. I have listed eight areas of contrast for discussion, namely money, drugs, setting new records, numbers competing, shoes, diet, water intake and television coverage. This list, however, is by no means exhaustive!

Money

By far the most dramatic and obvious difference in athletics between the early 1950s and today is simply money – money to equip and send teams abroad to the great international events and, more significantly, money received by the individual athletes generally.

With regard to the funding of teams, in order to keep the comparison of like with like as close as possible, I have selected the Empire and Commonwealth Games of 1954 and, 40 years later, the Commonwealth Games of 1994. Both were held in British Columbia, Canada, the former in the city of Vancouver and the latter in Victoria, Vancouver Island. My source data (statistics and quotations) have been drawn from the official Report by the BECG Council for

Scotland, 1954, and Neil Drysdale's article in *Scotland on Sunday*, 28 August 1994.

The following table that I have drawn up starkly and simply summarises the main differences:

	1954	*1994*
Team members (all sports)	22	176
Team members (athletics)	6	39
Officials (all sports)	4	49
Cost (all sports) (N.B. Balance in hand, afterwards:	£8,346-7/10d £2,321-14/-)	£1m
Cost (athletics)	included above	£75,000
Medals won (all sports)	6 Gold * 2 Silver 4 Bronze	6 Gold 3 Silver 11 Bronze
Medals won (athletics)	1 Gold 1 Bronze	1 Gold

*Note that bowling is not included in the table under 1954. The bowlers who represented Scotland had been touring Canada as part of a British Bowling Association team. They resided outwith the Empire Village and did not come under the scheme of general team arrangements. I never saw any of them. Their team figures were 7 bowlers, 1 official and 1 Bronze medal won.

The statistics in the above table speak for themselves; readers may draw their own conclusions! I would only make the obvious point that successes seem to be in inverse proportion to the numbers sent and money spent in 1994. One incidental fact, too, that does not appear in the table is that, despite the massive increase in the numbers of competitors sent in 1994, we had no male marathon runner. The lesson of 1954 had not been learned: no event is more unpredictable than the marathon!

These costs 40 years on, too, do not include sums spent, prior to the Games, on coaches, training camps at home and abroad, payments in grants to individual athletes, etc. Yet there seems to be no acknowledgement of comparative failure. The complacency, indeed, of those in charge is astonishing. Drysdale quotes Andy Vince, Scotland's director of athletics coaching in 1994: 'There's no need to be despondent about the way we've performed. In fact, I think we're doing superbly well.'! He also quotes Graeme Simmers, the chairman of the Scottish Sports Council, as declaring, 'Success, of course, should not be measured by medals alone,' a view categorically (and very sensibly!) denied by the party's principal sponsor, Edinburgh-based investment managers, Walter Scott and Partners: 'The objective of competitive sport is to win. Therefore, success for the Scottish team can only be gauged in terms of medals won.'

In this same article, however, Vince is also credited with an astonishing equating of medals with 'baubles'! 'There is always high expectation of medals by the sport itself, but the same people who wanted this team to return home with a hatful of baubles must surely appreciate that athletics has changed a great deal in recent seasons.' It certainly has!

One of these changes to which Vince is referring was the rise of African athletes to the top in athletic achievements. However, the attitude of many of these athletes soon shows where their priorities lie. In a discussion with David Moorcroft and Sue Barker on BBC at the time of the 1994 Commonwealth Games (27 August), Daley Thompson was quite blunt about it. They were discussing the semifinals of the 4 x 400 metres men's relay after the previous announcement of the disqualification of the Kenyan team. In particular, they were remarking on the absence of the top Kenyan athletes at the Games and, therefore, the relatively poor showing of Kenya generally, when Daley asserted, 'They want to spend all their time making money.'

Significantly, our sole success in Victoria, Yvonne Murray, who won the 10,000 metres gold medal, declared in an interview with Tom Knight (*Scotland on Sunday*, 28 August 1994): 'From 1990, I was forced to become a full-time athlete, and, as a professional, I had to pick races to support myself. The result was that I was running in races whether I was ready or not. I was too intense, too locked in on trying to succeed, trying to become the best 3,000 metres runner in the world and I sort of lost my way.' At least Yvonne was honest about it. She openly used the word 'professional' unlike the hypocrisy still manifest at times in references to Commonwealth and Olympic Games.

Don't get me wrong. I must make my own attitude clear. I don't object to athletes making money from their sport. I only wish that I had been able to do so. I certainly competed in the wrong era! Fifty years ago, I had to put just as much time and effort into my running and still cope with the demands of a full-time job. No, what I do decry was the mealy-mouthed hypocrisy then that deprived me from accepting any gift worth more than £11 from well-wishers and would have stripped me of my 'amateur' status for competing even unknowingly against a 'professional' or at a meeting not officially sanctioned by the association. So pernickety were some of these officials in interpreting their rules that for some time there was even a debate about banning school gym teachers from competing in amateur sport because their careers made them 'professionals'. Yet these teachers were some of the most important encouragers of sport among the young! However, in these cases, common sense eventually prevailed. Nevertheless, some of the interpretations of the rules could still be draconian. I knew, at that time, of young boys who had lost their chance of ever representing their country simply through unwittingly infringing one of these antiquated ordinances. I was lucky, I suppose. When still a schoolboy, I won the mile at a charity sports meeting at which I had been asked to run by one of the domestic science teachers at school. I made it clear that I could not accept a money prize, but later I was sent by post stamps worth 15/- (75p)! (my expenses?) There was nothing I could do about it. The village sports meeting was so obscure, however, that I was never 'found out' or my running career might never have even started. These rules – especially those applying to unregistered meetings – were so ridiculous that, if they had been applied absolutely strictly in every instance, I wonder whether even the great Eric Liddell would have made it to the Paris Olympics in 1924.

The great majority of our amateur athletic clubs were founded at the beginning of the last century by young men who were seeking fitness and fun as a respite from their drab working-class lives. Ironically, in drawing up their codes of conduct, they sought to embody in them the so-called, and largely mythical, Corinthian ideals of the gentleman sportsman of earlier centuries. Of course, in their attempts to keep their competitions free from the cheating and fraud caused by the influence of money, they were to a large extent justified in condemning the professional athletes of their day. Many of the old 'peds' ran in 'fixed' races, but, compared to today's competitors, they made negligible amounts of cash. Only the select few could earn enough money to make a living from their efforts. The actual money prizes were pitifully small and the money could be made mainly from betting. Under the aegis of wealthy sponsors – sometimes the bookmakers themselves – 'schools' of runners tried to predetermine the results of races. If a top runner were extremely fortunate, he might be subsidised for several weeks of preparation before a major race and yet, after a strenuous 'prep', find himself ordered to hold back in the actual race as his sponsor's money would be placed on another 'dark horse'.

To further their attempts to cheat, many 'peds' also adopted pseudonyms but even those who were genuine triers often adopted this practice to avoid the social stigma of professional running. My great-uncle, Jack Dickson, for example, who was a sprinter on the Lothians circuit in the 1920s until his business career took him to London, adopted his wife's name, Callaghan, whenever he competed.

It was, of course, much easier to cheat in the shorter races, especially the sprints, where the spectators could be easily conned, though it was not entirely impossible in the longer-distance races. Allan Scally, the top professional distance star of the late 1920s and early 1930s, who ran under his own name and was not involved in these dubious practices, used to tell of one runner who found himself so far ahead on the last lap at Powderhall that any holding back would have been glaringly obvious to the crowd of spectators. Suddenly, however, he retched and, with blood trickling down his chin, he staggered painfully on to be passed before the tape by the next man who was the one 'meant' to win. What the sympathetic punters did not see were the remains of the little phial of blood that he had bitten into!

Sometimes, the process would be reversed and a member of one of these 'schools' of runners would double-cross his confederates by genuinely going all out to win. Allan recalled one well-known 'ped' who ran under the pseudonym of 'The Monk' and who did precisely that at Bridge of Allan Games. He had arranged before the race for his brother to collect his clothing and, racing through the tape, he kept on running out of the Games field to avoid the inevitable retribution!

I personally witnessed some of these ploys as I stood near the finishing line at one of the earliest Camelon Mariners' Day sports. Two runners from the same 'school', who had obviously arranged to be first and second in the half-mile, were striding comfortably down the last straight when a young outsider suddenly sprinted past them. Seeing their plans thwarted, the runner who was meant to be second then put in a finishing burst past his colleague on whom their money was laid and managed to catch the young interloper on the line. It had been a desperately close finish and the crowd loved it. An inexperienced official, having handed the runners their place cards to take to the recorder's tent, then made the mistake of turning away. Immediately the winner turned to the young teenager and asserted, 'I certainly wasn't first. It was him,' and, pointing to his confederate, he handed him his first-place card. Then, taking the third-place card, he added 'and I was second' and grabbed the second-place card from the bemused youngster, who ended up with the third instead of the second-place card. Thus their original betting plan was reinstated!

I used the word 'hypocrisy' in referring to attitudes to amateur sport 50 years ago, but it was, however, nothing like the absurdities we see today. As I indicated earlier, I have no objections to athletes making money from their efforts, but why do we persist in using the word 'amateur' in our references to the sport from the Olympics down to lesser events at every level? No one can possibly deny that most of today's serious competitors are professionals in every sense of the word. Headlines like 'Athletes told to compete at indoor AAAs or lose money' (*Metro*, 23 December 2003) are grotesquely contradictory. (The first A = Amateur!) The article under this headline goes on to refer to 'promotional earnings and prize money'. Surely it would be much simpler and saner to omit the word 'amateur' entirely and refer just to 'athletes' and 'athletics'?

This constantly repeated refrain from many of our top athletes today is not a new phenomenon, however. Steve Cram in a Radio 4 broadcast on 26 August 1994 (discussing the drugs problem and the greater stress on athletes at that time), declared, 'A lot of them are professional athletes. They need to make a living ... Most of the British team are professional athletes and need to make a living.'

Two of the most notable athletes in the past decade, Linford Christie and Colin Jackson, made a very successful living. Under the punning headline 'Christie and Jackson maintain rich form', *The Scotsman* (20 August 1994) declared that Linford Christie (prior to going to the Commonwealth Games) 'has pocketed well over £250,000 from his sprinting exploits this year. When added to his many sponsorship deals, his yearly earnings have been boosted to about £1m.' Then, referring to the Grand Prix races (the 'Golden Four' meetings), it reported that both Christie and Jackson 'stayed in the hunt for a £160,000 jackpot at the Ivo Damme Memorial Grand Prix in Brussels', and explained that 'the prize awaiting the winners of selected events at all four (Grand Prix) is a stake in 20kg of gold ingot (worth an estimated $250,000)'. Note that this was in addition to prize money, appearance money, etc. In fact, at the Berlin Grand Prix, Jackson received a half-share in the gold bar (equalling £80,000).

Such an incentive to run for the money rather than the medals, then, is clearly overwhelming. Indeed, it was alleged at the time that Christie would not run for England in the Commonwealth relay or the 200 metres because it did not fit in with his training plans, but he did run in Italy on the day of the relay (and was beaten in the 100 metres by the American, Drummond). Yet Christie was team captain!

The following year, after Christie had suffered four defeats in his first five races, the *Radio Times* (5–11 August 1995) in a prominently featured article on Christie, mentioning his announced retiral by the end of the next season, claimed that 'he could not face defending his Olympic title in Atlanta next year', and stated that his win in the previous Olympics 'had made him a millionaire. When he won the World Championship the next year, his appearance fees shot through the roof – a matter of controversy with the British Athletics Federation, currently in dispute with Christie over his reported demand for £50,000 per race.'

Of course, such financial incentives were seen not only in Britain. *The Scotsman* (8 August 1996) referred to the 'Welcome Home' after the 1996 Atlanta Olympics received by medal winners and the consequent 'range of awards'. 'China made their Gold medallists millionaires in their local currency by way of cash gifts and perks. Australia coughed up £500,000 for their medallists.'

Top marathon runners too – especially after the advent of the big city marathons – had been reaping substantial financial rewards but more recently they really began to hit the jackpot. Under the headline 'Marathon Men Break Bank for Hero Haile', the *Metro* reported on 1 November 2001 that Haile Gebrselassie 'will pocket £350,000 when he makes his Flora London Marathon debut next year. The 28-year-old Ethiopian will enjoy what is reputedly athletics biggest-ever pay-day for his first race over 26.2 miles ...

But organisers are sure the double Olympic champion will justify the mammoth outlay and insist he could even go for a world record. "The fee is probably the biggest-ever paid in athletics and certainly the most we have paid for an athlete," admitted the race organiser, David Bedford ... And Bedford added, "I always said that if it was a question of money, then Haile's debut would be in London."'

At the time of the following London Marathon (April 2003), writing in *Marathon News* (the official magazine of the Flora London Marathon), Neil Wilson of the *Daily Mail* quoted this most significant comment by Alan Storey, a leading coach and technical consultant to the London race: 'Ten years ago, there were six, eight, maybe even ten marathons that could afford some of the best runners. Now not even New York figures highly in their minds. If any runner thinks there may be a world record in them, they go where their chances are best and the rewards are greatest.' Is it at all surprising, therefore, that some of these 'elite' runners are not all that interested in representing their countries and competing for medals in international championships?

Even when athletes do compete for championship medals, however, the financial rewards afterwards can be very lucrative – as we have already seen in the post-Atlanta Olympic reports. It is obvious that the old idea of the amateur being an unpaid part-timer has long since gone for both men and women.

Ironically, financial pressures are now being offered as excuses for injuries and poor performances. Referring to the worry of Jonathan Edwards' ankle injury and the definite withdrawals of other athletes from the British squad for the World Championships, the UK athletics performance director, Max Jones, lamented that 'the last 18 months have been very tough for our athletes. The pressure to perform at their peak to pay their mortgages, bills, travelling and training puts a lot of stress on the individual.' (*Metro*, 20 August 2003).

I could go on and on quoting instances of athletes today bemoaning the levels of financial sponsorship available to them and their problems with money – even before some of them have fully established themselves.

'Then and Now'? No further comment is needed by me! Then we were amateurs in the sense that we could not make a living from our sport. Now they are professionals who expect to earn a very good living, to pay their mortgages, etc.

A final postscript on the sheer ridiculousness of trying to distinguish between the terms 'amateur' and 'professional': on 15 August 2005, Paula Radcliffe, in a radio interview after her magnificent win in the World Championships Marathon in Helsinki the day before, was asked about why the rest of the athletics team did so badly and what could be done for the future and she used the word 'professional' three times in one sentence in her reply.

Drugs

When money (and so much money!) is at stake, then it is inevitable that the temptation to use drugs to enhance performance becomes very strong. The need to win at all costs becomes imperative. Steve Cram in the radio broadcast that I mentioned earlier, when he emphasised the stress that afflicted many athletes who were professionals and needed to make a living out of the sport, was discussing the seriousness of the drug problem a decade ago.

Two days later, Neil Drysdale in his article in *Scotland on Sunday* (28 August 1994), reported: 'Before the Commonwealth Games had even started, Professor Peter Radford, the executive chairman of the British Athletics

Federation, summed up the principal difficulty in tackling the drug issue which has reared its head with the advent of every major championship in the 1990s. "It is a matter of public record. There are athletes out there who think they need stimulants to produce winning performances, and anyone who believes that the drug-taking will stop is living in cloud-cuckoo land."

Even then, however, it was not a new phenomenon. That same day, David Moorcroft, commenting on BBC1 on the Commonwealth Games, spoke of 'the hypocrisy of the last 20 years'. He was visibly moved and referred to some, probably drug-takers themselves, who were now retired and pontificating on the problem.

Since then, despite the increasing and more rigorous use of testing procedures and bans of varying degrees of severity on those testing positively, there have been highly publicised cases. Indeed, it has been said that some of those found guilty of such cheating (for make no bones about it, trying to gain an unfair advantage over one's fellow competitors in this way is cheating) have even been talking of possible legal action on the grounds of loss of earnings! These anti-drugs measures, however, are still not deterring even those at the highest level. I am glad, therefore, to see the decision in America to prosecute coaches who supply the steroids and other drugs to their charges. This type of action might be more effective in trying to stamp out the practice.

No matter how rigorous the investigations and testing programmes might be, these attempts cannot keep pace with the efforts to produce ever-more-refined and effective (and, above all, undetectable!) stimulants. I am afraid that I must agree with Professor Radford's rather pessimistic conclusion ten years ago. When so much money and prestige (with its consequent commercial benefits) can be gained, there will always be those willing to take the risk.

There are those, too, who would try to defend the indefensible – one radio pundit even arguing that the motive for an athlete taking drugs might simply be the desire to keep up with his fellow competitors, who, he suspects, are all already doing so. If this is true, then the situation would really be hopeless!

The contrast with half a century ago could not have been more striking. We certainly lived in an entirely different world. Harriers never dreamed of drug-taking and regarded it as detrimental to the health and well-being we were striving for. The only food additive I ever took was a spoonful of glucose powder, which I added to the water I used to gulp down after finishing a long training run in the heat of midsummer.

Of course, we were not beguiled by the prospect of making money. To the professional athlete of today, a ban from competition of a couple of years might spell financial ruin. Paradoxically, if a ban had been inflicted in our day for whatever reason (certainly not for drug-taking, I hasten to add!), it might even have had positive results. You could have kept training hard without the stress of competition or worrying about financial consequences and then returned reinvigorated to surprise everyone in your next race!

Setting New Records

The phenomenal changes in records are what we might expect over a period of 50 years of steadily increasing professionalism. Until the 1930s, the 'magic barrier' for marathon runners in championship races was 2½ hours. Then Kitei Son recorded 2hrs 29mins 19.2secs in the 1936 Berlin Olympics, but, even after the war, Cabrera's winning time in the 1948 London Olympics was still almost 2hrs 35mins (2hrs 34mins 51.6secs). Compare this with the

London Marathon times of today – almost half an hour faster! Then, beginning in 1951 with 2hrs 31mins 42.6secs in the AAA Championship, Jim Peters set increasingly faster times in 1952 and 53 until he shattered the 2hrs 20mins barrier with a new world record of 2hrs 17mins 29.4secs in 1954.

I used the phrase 'magic barrier', but, perhaps, 'psychological barrier' would have been a more accurate term. Once one man proved that it could be broken, the new record became merely the norm and runner after runner followed suit until the present times of around 2hrs 5mins are being achieved. The same phenomenon was demonstrated by Bannister in the mile. Once the four-minute barrier had been broken, it was done again and again and the record was drastically reduced. In the marathon, instead of running comparatively easily for the first 20 miles or so and leaving the final all-out effort till the closing miles, Jim now showed that one could start fast and keep it up all the way.

The difference, therefore, between today's runners and ourselves half a century ago was one of expectations. Speaking for myself and for my fellow competitors at that time, with the possible exception of Jim Peters, our main concern was to win the race and not to set a new record. If the latter came, it was a bonus – simply a by-product. The obsession today with setting record times, however, is clearly demonstrated by the practice (anathema in the past!) of not only allowing but paying top-class pacemakers to lead the race until they drop out at the half-marathon distance and by offering fantastically rich prizes for a new world record.

Only once did I consciously set out to break a record – my reduction of the 1929 North Berwick to Edinburgh record by almost 34 minutes being a deliberate attempt to gain publicity for Empire and Commonwealth Games selection. In all my other races, I ran solely to beat the opposition and did enough to win. Nevertheless, unsure of the power of my finish (despite my increasingly successful final sprints), I rarely left my flat-out effort till the very end and this tactic probably brought me the record times I did achieve. As a schoolboy, I envied the way John Joe Barrie, the Irish track star, could ease past his rivals on the tape. I remember feeling exhilarated by being just beaten by him in a one-mile race, only to see him doing exactly the same to Andy Forbes, the National Three Miles champion, in his next race. No, I followed rather the axiom of Jim Flockhart, a fellow Shettleston Harrier and Scotland's only international cross-country champion pre-war – 'If you can beat a man by 500 yards, then do so. Don't leave it to just five yards. Next time, he will not offer you such a tough race.' My only concern in a race, indeed, as I have described earlier, was not with my own time but with the time-gap between myself and the man behind me.

Comparing athletes from widely separated decades solely on the basis of times recorded is never entirely valid. If the runners of 50 years ago were competing today, who knows what times we might achieve? Certainly, my motivation and training then can stand comparison with those of today's professionals, but we had to work full-time as well in order to earn our living and did not have all the luxurious advantages such as acclimatisation camps abroad, etc. Far be it from me to claim that I would have been among the present elite, but I am sure at least that I would have been much closer to their times. There certainly would not have been the almost 20-minute gap between my best marathon time and today's records. I am not speaking solely for myself. When Chris Brasher used to stir up arguments at the London Marathon's 'Notable

Nineteen' dinners as to why Britain was achieving so little medal success in the marathon at recent championships, I would look round the table at the array of past medal winners and feel certain that, if they were running now, they would have been more than capable of holding their own. They beat the best of their eras. Who could be expected to do more?

My own answer to Chris's question would be to point to the advantages enjoyed by even the most energetically inclined young people today. They have the opportunities to engage in so many (but so much more expensive!) sports such as golf, tennis, skiing, even bowls or curling and sometimes their energies and interests are dissipated by participating in several. We had neither the money nor the facilities and, perforce, could not be other than single-minded in our pursuit of the cheapest sport of all – running on the public roads.

Numbers Competing

An obvious change from 50 years ago is the sheer numbers competing in distance races – not so much perhaps in the cross-country championships but in the city marathons. In my day, we could have a field of several hundred in the big cross-country events, and, though you might be first runner for your team with the other team members lined up in single file behind you, even on racecourses it could still be a hazardous fight in the first mad rush. Often, indeed, you were aiming for a narrow gap leading off the grass and on to narrow paths through trees and bushes.

It was quite different, however, in the marathons 50 years ago when the entries were much smaller. The biggest field I encountered was in my second attempt at the full-distance race in the Polytechnic Harriers marathon and Olympic trial in May 1952, when nearly 200 runners lined up in two rows in the spacious grounds of Windsor Castle preparatory to starting the race to Chiswick. I, nevertheless, had to report for a medical check just before the start. Imagine trying to vet everyone starting in the London Marathon today!

The biggest field in Scotland at that time would be about 50 and no difficulties of crowding were ever encountered at the start. In those days too, no one under 21 was allowed to compete and no women were allowed either. Now, in the London Marathon, the numbers have risen to around 34,000. The elite runners line up at the front but so dense is the crowd stretching away behind them that little more than a shuffling walk can be possible for quite some time for those in the midst of the throng, and by then the top runners will be well underway. Several minutes at least may elapse even before those at the back cross the actual start line. Most of them, however, are not too worried about the niceties of timing, except perhaps beating their own time in the same race and under the same conditions as in previous years. Their main ambition is to finish the 26 miles. The enforced slowness of the start, indeed, is probably a blessing in disguise for these 'fun' runners, preventing them from 'blowing up' early in the race.

The novice with more serious ambitions for achieving success at the full marathon distance, however, is faced with quite a problem. Having no previous recorded marathon time to declare, they will find themself buried among the thousands of 'fun' runners (or even perhaps not have their entry accepted!), and their finishing time, they might feel, could have been faster for the purpose of quoting on their next entry for the race. For such a runner, the best plan would be to record a time at a much smaller event before attempting the big city marathon.

In Scotland, the numbers running in the city marathons in the 1980s at the height of the marathon popularity were much smaller than those in cities like London, New York or Tokyo, but, nevertheless, were still huge compared with those in the 1950s and the sheer size of the entries presented problems we never encountered. The experience of my son, Joe, for example, was a salutary one. He ran in the Edinburgh Marathon in the early 1980s in a field of around 4,000. He was a very good runner, but, like the vast majority of his fellow competitors that day, he had never ever run the full distance before, even in training. As a boy, he used to cover up to 12 miles with me, but in training for this race he had never run more than six miles. Using his natural speed, he fought his way clear of the crowds of 'fun' runners after leaving the Queen's Park outside Holyrood Palace and soon latched on to the leading bunch. He then managed to stay with them for 20 miles before, inevitably, the dreaded 'knock' hit him and he was reduced to a walking pace over those last gruelling six miles. However, when Meadowbank Stadium came into sight, he revived and began to run again. Indeed, he managed to put in a strong finish down the track. Considering how slowly he had covered those last six miles, his marathon time (below 3½ hours) was very creditable. He had then to rush off for his afternoon hospital duties shift, but, extremely sore and muscle-bound, he could not return to work for the next two days! The tragic outcome was that his experience, like that of so many others, put him off marathon running completely and he never attempted the full distance again. It simply reinforced a basic tenet of my own philosophy of marathon running: psychologically, you must know that you can last the 26 miles and this means that you should have covered at least the full distance or more on easy training runs before you ever attempt to race.

In Scotland, the logistical and financial problems involved with the huge numbers of competitors eventually caused the demise of these big city marathons and their replacement with half-marathons. By contrast, our organisational problems in the 1950s were infinitesimal and yet the authorities then would not even allow us to run along Edinburgh's Princes Street in our finish towards Meadowbank Stadium and insisted that the route had to detour via Leith. They also had a rule enforcing at any stage of the race the withdrawal of any runner falling more than half an hour behind the leader. I don't know whether the rule had been rescinded by the time I drastically reduced the record, but it certainly could be rather unfair, depending upon how fast the winner ran from year to year. If such a rule were to be applied in today's races, literally many thousands would not be allowed to finish!

Psychological pressures were also applied (unintentionally, perhaps) in our day. I remember following the race from Falkirk to Edinburgh in the runners' bus one year when I was still too young to enter. We passed the last runner at Linlithgow Bridge only five miles into the race. He was obviously having a bad spell and, deciding to take things cannily, he was quite some distance behind the pack. An ambulance, however, was crawling along right on his heels!

Shoes

For me personally, the most important difference between these two very different eras proved to be not money but, it may sound absurd, shoes. If I had had the latest lightweight, aerodynamic training shoes available today, I would still have been able to run. I had anticipated going on enjoying a run in the countryside – at much gentler speeds, of course – until well into old age. Others like

Emmet Farrell, indeed, had continued to do so into their 90s. I had been fortunate to have been able to go running with my son, Joe, but I would dearly love to accompany my grandchildren, who show real promise and talent at the sport. Alas, the crippling pains of osteoarthritis in both knees finally forced me to call it a day when I was 65 after I had struggled on intermittently for almost 15 years. A contributory cause could have been the fact that I had run for years in all weathers with no covering at all on my knees and lower legs but the main cause undoubtedly was the type of shoes I was forced to wear in my running.

When I first began pounding out the miles on the road, the only shoes I could get were either thin plimsolls (hard inner-soled gym shoes) or Dunlop cushioned tennis shoes, which were really too heavy to use in races. Finally, I managed to obtain a light gym shoe with a thin layer of cushioning, which cost the princely sum of 12 shillings and sixpence, and it was these I wore (with my feet liberally coated in Vaseline to prevent blistering!) in the Vancouver race. I discussed the problem of shoes with the volunteer driver who ferried me round the Vancouver course prior to the race. It chanced that he was a shoe manufacturer and he presented me later with his latest design – tennis shoes with a special cut-out at the instep on the outside of the soles to promote flexibility. Like the Dunlop ones, however, they also proved to be too heavy and, in addition, rather tight.

When I returned home from Canada, I was informed that the German sports company, Adidas, had been given permission to send their latest spiked track shoes to each of the gold medallists. I asked for road shoes and received a pair of the first black-and-white-striped Adidas trainers to be seen in this country. Unfortunately, unlike today's shoes, the soles, though cushioned, were still flat like the plimsolls I used. Nevertheless, proud of my new acquisition,

I foolishly wore them at once on a 20-mile run and lost both big toe-nails! It was the uppers this time that caused the bother and, needless to say, it was the last time I risked wearing them on long runs.

My last attempt to get something a bit better than the plimsolls was to make a drawing of my foot and send it to the English firm, Fosters. Their lightweight shoes had soft kangaroo leather uppers and a cushioning though the soles, inner and outer, again were simply flat. I wore them in my last two championship wins but, carefully watching the expense, I saved them purely for races and continued for years pounding out my training in the old-fashioned plimsolls. Money, or should I say the lack of it, was still the deciding factor!

Jim Peters faced the same difficulty with shoes. Indeed, to cut down on the expense, he went far further. Both of us had mentioned the problem in a memorable Radio 5 Live interview in April 1996, and Jim later said that he even used to switch round his shoes when they became worn, wearing the right on the left foot and vice-versa, to make them last longer. It seems incredible but it was another instance of how much he was capable of punishing himself and ignoring pain!

When my osteoarthritis was diagnosed in Aberdeen in the early 1980s, I bought an exercise cycle and, stripped to the waist, used to hammer away on it, recording 25 miles an hour. It certainly seemed to keep me fit until the inevitable happened. After a good many 1,000 miles, the bike fell apart and I (suffering now from saddle-soreness!) decided against buying another. Instead, having now moved back to Edinburgh, I tried running again, combined with three-hour walks at the weekends. Gradually, I built up my runs round the Braid and Pentland Hills to over ten miles but the latest and most expensive training shoes

I could buy had come too late for me. The pains in my knees worsened eventually to the extent that I could not take a running stride forward and I was forced to stop. However, I then bought a mini-trampoline and found that, using music to maintain my rhythm, I was able to run on the spot indoors and, weather permitting, in the garden. The biggest drawback here (as with the exercise cycle) was simply the sheer monotony of the task that rapidly became a grind and not a pleasure!

Diet

I am amused at today's emphasis on special diets for marathon runners and especially the practice of stocking up on cereals and other foods rich in carbohydrates immediately prior to a race.

I ate whatever I wanted – or could get! (Rationing had not long ended.) Expending so much energy in combining work and training, I always had a pretty good appetite. Indeed, in my RAF officer course when part of our work involved our being trained as infantry officers, I was always hungry despite the food being excellent both in quality and quantity. (Of course, after an often-strenuous day in the field, I was trying at the same time to fit my running into the little free time we had in the evenings.) I even resorted to keeping stocks of bread and marmalade (sent by my dad in a parcel with laundry from home!) hidden in a compartment in my boot locker. I certainly had no fads about special foods.

The more solid the fare, indeed, the better I liked it, especially after training. After an ultra-long run such as the 30-plus miles that I used to run on New Year's Day, however, a curious thing happened. I would come home absolutely ravenous and my mum would have prepared steak pie and generous helpings of thick rice, but, after eating comparatively little (for me!), I found that I felt very full. I used to say that, having covered such a distance, my stomach must have shrunk!

I learned the hard way, however, to be careful about what I ate immediately before a race. My first attempt at the Scottish Marathon title was in 1952 when the course was from Almondbank, then through Perth and on to Dundee. Lunch was laid on for us in a Perth restaurant and I chose what I thought was the most innocuous dish – boiled fish. It proved to be too much and too close to the start and I certainly suffered for it. My stomach felt as if it were tied in knots for the first 13 miles before I began to settle. Then I made an effort and at 15 miles I caught up with the leader and eventual winner, Charlie Robertson of Dundee. It had been a foolish spurt, however, and I paid for it over the last six miles. In the end I finished fifth.

Thereafter, I was careful prior to a race, carrying my own sandwiches if I had to travel a distance from home to the start or eating scrambled eggs and toast at home if the venue was not too far away. The principle I acted upon was simple: viz. to eat something light enough not to disturb me during the race but sufficient enough to last me over the full distance and prevent the dreaded 'knock' over the closing miles.

Eventually, I found myself adopting the same practice for training and keeping my solid main meal until the evening. At RAF Turnhouse, at morning coffee break in the officers' mess, they served the most delicious hamburger rolls simply dripping with fried onions. I succumbed to the temptation several times before resolutely avoiding the mess in mid-morning. I found that it was playing havoc with my run at lunchtime when most of my serious training took place. I therefore used to eat light sandwiches, cheese or banana, with a pint of milk, sitting at my desk an hour or so before my 15-mile run. Then, one day, after a bout of nausea had forced me to shorten my run, I cut out the milk and from then on settled for tea.

What (and when) I ate, therefore, was simply a matter of common-sense personal experimentation to find what did not interfere with my regular running. It was never the case of using the often prohibitively expensive food supplements such as are advertised in the sports magazines today.

Water Intake

Closely linked to the question of diet is the problem of water intake both in training and races. In training, I only once ever accepted a drink – from a housewife watching with her children on a very hot day as I toiled uphill past her country cottage on one of the back roads between Slamannan and Bathgate. In races, too, there was only the one occasion – the AAA Marathon Championship at Cardiff in 1953 – when I took on liquid and, as I described earlier, I then lost interest in the race. At the water stations in races (approximately every five miles), I never drank but simply grabbed the water to splash over my face as I ran past without breaking stride. Even the awful warning of Jim Peters's collapse in the heat of Vancouver (after which the doctor told me that he had never seen anyone so completely dehydrated) did not cause me to deviate from my policy of abstaining from drinking during my runs.

On my training runs, I never carried the now seemingly obligatory water bottle. It was simply too clumsy and awkward as, on my many runs home from work, I had to carry a handkerchief wrapped round a small wallet with my money, watch and sometimes even my gold pen. However, I would never have taken a drink anyway, as I dared not risk being caught out without a place to relieve myself. The roads over which I trained offered few, if any, opportunities for the necessary privacy. The villages and towns through which I passed seemed to be singularly lacking in toilet facilities. On extremely long runs, my only chances of a much-needed 'pit-stop' were either in a few secluded spots in the wilds of the hills or the even fewer roadside pockets of woodland. I therefore trained myself simply to avoid taking water in.

In races, too, 50 years ago, this same problem of lack of toilet facilities was to be encountered (unlike the plethora of portable 'loos' today!). Even if the rare public toilet came into sight, however, I could not afford the precious time spent in relieving myself. I dared not risk losing contact with my rivals immediately round me or, worse still, allow those behind me to catch up. Gulping down water at the various water stations would only have aggravated my discomfort and also increased the craving for more fluid. In the years since then, I have often been asked how much I drank during a race and my reply, 'Not a drop!' has been met with incredulity.

I do not deny at all the dangers of dehydration – my own experience with weight loss after my third Scottish Championship victory was, as I described earlier, severe enough – but, since then, the precautions have been taken to ridiculous extremes. With the advent of the marathon-running boom, 'experts' advocated the constant intake of water to combat the loss of body fluids and, in the big races, commercial manufacturers of 'energy drinks' even began to distribute free samples to the competitors. Their advice, however, has been taken to absurd lengths. I regularly see many joggers plodding past my house awkwardly clutching their precious bottles even on the coldest of days and some of them at least on obviously the shortest of runs.

'Expert' opinion, however, seems to be veering round again. *Metro* carried an article by Suzanne Stevenson (5

June 2003) warning joggers that drinking too much can be bad for them. She quoted David Martin, a top US exercise physiologist (Georgia State University) investigating illness in 'fun-runners': 'Instead of holding a bottle and swigging at every opportunity, it's best to drink only when you are thirsty. Too much water can cause hyponatraemia or water intoxication – where the blood is diluted so much that sodium levels fall, causing dizziness and breathing problems.' Since 1985, he had discovered 70 cases (more than those suffering from dehydration!). 'The problem affects slower runners rather than elite athletes who are running too fast to drink much. [The very point I made earlier!] Joggers could be in danger of becoming lethargic from drinking too much, not from running too much.' His conclusion is vehement: 'We are worried about people taking up running for the first time and who are told, "You can't drink too much." That's wrong, wrong, wrong.'

More significantly, in this country, as Suzanne Stevenson points out, Martin's argument is supported by the Flora London Marathon's medical director, Dr Dan Tunstall-Pedoe: 'Long-distance, slower runners in particular are taking in huge amounts, in some cases up to two pints per hour. Many end up collapsing after the race and going to hospital. Women are particularly vulnerable as a water bottle has become a fashion accessory.' (!!) (His recommendation was less than a pint per hour of exercise and slightly more on hot days.) Perhaps, my own practice was not so bad after all!

Television Coverage

I must applaud the quantity and quality of the television reporting of today's athletics events, and yet I find myself asking, 'Do I really enjoy the colourful spectacle as much as I did in the 1950s when the old black-and-white coverage, often hazy especially in the evenings, made for much more difficult viewing?'

Certainly, the most exciting programme I ever watched was the fantastic duel between the Russian Kuts and Chris Chataway when a new world 5,000 metres record of 13mins 51.8secs was set on an October evening in 1954 in London. Our living room in Falkirk was packed with friends round our 12-inch black-and-white TV and, during that amazing last lap when Chataway passed Kuts on the last five yards of the three miles, 160 yards, I found myself literally standing on a chair yelling him home.

The technical quality of today's TV coverage of athletics is, of course, quite superb by comparison. I eagerly watch the Olympics and the World Championships and I love especially the spectacle of the London Marathon, but I wonder, when we consider the big city evening meetings, if, perhaps, the sport is now being over-exposed. I find myself curiously unmoved and even reluctant at times to settle down and watch the latter. This may be due in part to the use of paid pacemakers, which I have already mentioned, for, though the chances of new records are enhanced, much of the thrill of the race between genuine triers for me is distorted. I have already made it abundantly clear that I am not against money prizes, but, if the organisers would cut down on (or even cut out) 'appearance money', there would be a greater incentive to run to win and the result would make for better races. We might then see fewer of those 'stars', who are highly paid to appear, failing to live up to expectations.

The prima donna histrionics of some of the 'stars', moreover, can be distinctly off-putting, and the dominance of commercial interests influencing the sport is also clearly a possibility. On the 8 August 1994, for example, *The Scotsman* reported that Leroy Burrell, the 100 metres world record holder, finished in seventh place behind Christie in the Zürich Grand Prix the night before. The TV report carried the astonishing comment, 'Burrell's manager manipulated things to get him into the final when he did not qualify in the semis.'

On occasion, too, I cringe at hearing the sycophantic and even downright silly remarks by some television sports commentators (not all, I hasten to add), often recently retired athletes (and a few still active) who become overnight media 'experts'. The ease with which the latter achieve these various 'jobs for the boys' (and girls!) contrasts markedly with the situation in the 1950s. I remember writing at that time to the BBC about the possibility of obtaining employment – only to receive the brief and unnecessarily curt reply that all their posts were advertised in the press. (Despite my closest scrutiny of the newspapers, I never saw one!) They ignored my credentials – the fact that I had achieved the highest marks in speech work at Jordanhill Training College and in the RAF, and that I had, indeed, already performed creditably and fluently in live interviews on both TV and radio.

I have discussed at some length, then, the major contrasts with half a century ago, enough, at least, to show how athletes of my generation lived in an entirely different world. What, however, did we have that is missing to a large extent today? Briefly, I would say, a love and enjoyment of running for its own sake and not for any material benefits that we might get out of it. But that is a theme I will develop much more fully in the later chapter, 'Per Ardua Ad?'.

Chapter 16

Advice for Aspiring Marathon Runners

MANY BEGINNERS inspired by the example of champions try to follow their training programmes and soon succumb to injuries or give up in disgust at not achieving the hoped-for dramatic results. Therefore the first and most important basic principle is to avoid slavishly copying some top athletes' training schedules. They may have brought them success but they will almost certainly not work for you, a beginner. You don't know the previous running they may have done to build up the background of fitness that underpins their now rigorous schedules. You must find through personal experiment what will suit you best. International runners, to whom I have already referred, New Zealand's Mike Ryan and South Africa's Tommy Malone, I am proud to say, were spurred on as youths by my own example, but the training schedules they devised as champions were their own.

Therefore, start by trying to run as often as you can in the time available. I began simply by determining that, as I could not then match my fellow competitors for speed, I would do more work and achieve a higher mileage than anyone else. Ignore the stopwatch to begin with. Run gently for as far as you can and still feel comfortable. You will soon find yourself running easily over much longer distances than you thought possible. Above all, the experience must be a pleasant one. Go out to enjoy the sun and the scenery. I cannot stress too much the importance of these long easy runs. If you compete over shorter distances for your club, you will be astonished at how your times in such races have improved without having done any specific speed work. My own record times over five miles in the Nigel Barge Memorial race and the six miles in the Edinburgh to Glasgow Relay and my winning international cross-country recognition were achieved on the basis of long easy marathon runs. Fartlek-type training, alternating fast all-out bursts and slower intermediate striding, is best undertaken only when you have already reached and demonstrated peak fitness and success. Finally, I cannot overemphasise the importance, both physical and psychological, of having covered the full marathon distance frequently in training before attempting to tackle the major marathon races.

The psychological benefits of simply logging every run and seeing the mileage steadily mount up are extremely important. The sense of achievement will do much to boost your self-confidence. I obtained an exercise-type quarto notebook, lined it off in columns and devoted a double-page spread to each week's training. The left-hand page had four columns headed 'Date', 'Course', 'Approx. Distance' and 'Time' with the widest column devoted to 'Course'. The facing page had a narrow column headed 'Conditions' and a much wider space devoted to 'Remarks'. At the end of each week (Sunday to Saturday), I drew a line across both pages and at the very foot of the left-hand page, I noted the total mileage for the week. As 'Saturday' was the final entry on the page, I had more space to note the results of races, which, at that time, always took place on Saturdays, and it was handy for quick reference. At the back of the book, I fitted into a single line the week number and date, the mileage covered and the cumulative total, the number of runs and their cumulative total and the number of days per week and their cumulative total. A single page held 26 weeks of these statistics. It was essential to note at least the most important of these details for each training session as soon as possible after each run. I found that leaving it off for even only a few days made it extremely difficult to remember especially as I was attempting to run every day.

Although I recorded my time for almost every run, I never ran against the clock nor tried to set new record times for the route (though, of course, inevitably they did occur!). Indeed, just by glancing at my 'Conditions' (wind direction, etc.) and 'Remarks' ('medium-even pace', for example), I was able to compare my times for two apparently identical runs over the same course and note the often dramatic improvement over a period of a few weeks. Moreover, Arthur Newton's views regarding the inadvisability of continually setting oneself time trials in training were invaluable to me. I liked especially his analogy of putting money into the bank. You don't keep on withdrawing it every week simply to prove that it's there!

Many beginners will probably have joined an athletic club and may find themselves chosen for one of the teams the club will enter in races, often every other week throughout the winter season especially. It is important that you regard these races simply as part of your long-term training programme and avoid trying to 'peak' with every race. This is essentially a mental quality. Though I certainly did my best in these intermediate, often quite short, cross-country and road races, I tried never to become despondent at my performance. I never regarded these events as ends in themselves. Their value was that of adding to my mileage and, as well as warming up for a mile or so before the start, I often ran on for an easy mile or more after the finish in order to boost my total further. Indeed, sometimes I would go out for a normal easy training run in the morning before leaving home for one of these races in the afternoon.

By all means train, if possible, with other fellow club members. Their company, especially on long runs, can certainly make the miles fly past. However, do not be dependent on the whims of these training partners. Their attitudes to bad weather, to take only one example, may be quite different, and the strength of their resolve to keep training every day may be much weaker than your own. Although I have stressed time and time again the essential quality of enjoyment, paradoxically what distinguishes the champion from the average runner is that they keep training on many occasions when they don't feel like it! I often had to force myself to go out, particularly when the weather was bad but, once I had a mile or so behind me, I was fine.

Although I may appear to be emphasising the single-mindedness, which is an essential quality for the potential champion, nevertheless I am certainly not advocating a completely blinkered attitude to other – more important – interests in life. I remember the remarks of a workmate of my father with whom I used to sit and eat my lunchtime sandwiches during my student vacation work in ICI Grangemouth. Alec Stuart seriously advocated that, having graduated and proved myself academically, I should now devote myself exclusively, full-time and for some years, to the sport at which I was already showing promise. I am glad to say that I did not even attempt to follow this advice. I decided as far as possible to try to fit my training into the normal routine pattern of my life. I would run at lunchtimes and back from work (thus saving both time and bus fares!) and still manage to join in social activities like the dramatic club, theatre entertainments, dances, etc. (and later, of course, courting!). Indeed, I remember, for example, one working day covering in a couple of outings the equivalent of the full marathon distance and then rushing off to the annual school dance in the evening.

Finally, I must stress again, don't be in a hurry to compete in major races until you have established a solid background of slowish runs over the full marathon. Get the confidence of knowing that you can last every mile. Then, having entered, run your own style of race. Run, of course, with the aim to win (or, at least, to run better than you have managed before), but do not be overconcerned with times. Setting new records should always be secondary to victory. Remember, too, that, when you begin to feel bad (as you almost inevitably will in every race), you must not give way to despair. Console yourself with the thought that the other runners at your elbow or in front of you are probably feeling worse!

Chapter 17

Per Ardua Ad?

'THROUGH HARDSHIPS to what?' Towards the end of 1950, I used the above part of the RAF motto as the title of an article I submitted to the Jordanhill Training College magazine. After graduating from Glasgow University that summer, I had enrolled for a year's teacher-training at Jordanhill. To help out a classmate of mine in the English course, who was editing the college magazine, I wrote a piece about why anyone would want to run a marathon and tried to describe in some detail what it felt like. At that time, I had never competed in a marathon. You had to be over 21 before they would allow you to enter and I had just reached that age. My article was not entirely based on imagination, however. I had followed the Scottish Championship race in the competitors' bus and had listened avidly to Joe Walker's anecdotes of past events – especially his account of his visit to the Berlin Olympics in 1936 and his praise for the superb camera work on the epic marathon between Kitei Son and Ernie Harper.

My classmate, rather cruelly and frivolously I thought, repaid my efforts by ruining the continuity of my article by dividing it into parts and using it as a linking device throughout the magazine. After a few paragraphs, he commented, 'He's off! Turn to page such and such.' Then he proceeded to ridicule some of my certainly more lurid descriptions by satirical remarks and innuendo. When, for example, in describing the sufferer's extremity of thirst, I wrote something like, 'His whole body craves only one thing,' he would interpolate, 'Tut, tut, Joe!'

Now I suppose my descriptions seemed rather melodramatic and high-flown at the time, but, only a very few years later, they were to prove astonishingly prophetic and, indeed, understated when I think of the tortures Jim Peters underwent in the Empire and Commonwealth Games and, to a lesser extent, my own sufferings in the heat in my other championship wins. After Vancouver, my paraphrasing of Kipling's lines in my article did not seem too exaggerated:

If you can force your heart and nerve and sinew
To serve your turn long after they have gone
And so hold on when there is nothing in you
Except the Will which says to them: 'Hold on!'
… You'll be a marathon Man, my son!

My article had perhaps been only too successful in describing the pains and tribulations besetting the marathon runner or, indeed, in indicating the qualities of character needed, but I doubt if it produced any really successful answer to the question: 'Why inflict such punishment upon oneself?'

At that time, the answer was certainly not financial gain. As I made clear in a previous chapter, 50 years ago athletics was an entirely different world and money simply did not enter into our consideration of the question, unlike in some instances today where money rather than medals or patriotism seems to be the main motivation. Nevertheless, even then I was often asked by the man in the street,

'How much money do you make out of it?' When I used to answer, 'Not a penny. I'm frequently out of pocket,' I was at once met with the incredulous query, 'Why? You must be daft to do so much monotonous work without being paid anything for it.' 'Daft?' A doctor once asked a fellow marathoner why he wanted a medical examination (a requirement for entry for certain races). On being told that my friend was about to race 26 miles, the doctor briefly replied, 'It's not your heart I should be examining, it's your head!' Sometimes, I felt almost inclined to agree with him when I tried to answer, 'Why?'

It certainly was not a desire for fame (or notoriety!) either. In fact, in my own case, if I had been so inclined, I would have been disappointed. In many references to the Vancouver Marathon in the media, my name is not even mentioned or it is stuck in as an afterthought. Not for nothing did one tabloid newspaper dub me 'the forgotten man'. Sometimes, however, whatever recognition there might be of my name had even an adverse effect. Weeks after I had achieved a promotion to another school, for example, I was told by a member of the appointing committee visiting my new school that, before they had even seen me, most of the committee had been prejudiced against me. 'They thought your brains were all in your feet!' However, my interview performance had saved the day. Thereafter, I was distinctly chary of mentioning my sporting achievements! At another interview for a PR post with an American oil company, I was told bluntly to forget my athletics ambitions. All my time had to be devoted to their interests. Their attitude seemed to be that I was to be theirs body and soul. That effectively ended any inclination I might have had to change from a career in education to one in business.

People often said to me that all that running must have been a very good way of keeping fit. It certainly was (injuries excepted)! The sense of physical power and well-being in pitting one's abilities against others, the discovery that, after running ten miles, for example, one could produce a burst of speed faster than anything one could have produced from scratch – these were some of the rewards of all one's hard training. But the real victory was over oneself: in many races, at some stage or other, the battle was not against others but against the great temptation to give up and it was here that the self-discipline, acquired in one's lonely hours of training, triumphed in the resulting success when all the pains were then forgotten.

These benefits of physical fitness and mental discipline, however, were in one sense only a by-product of running in the first place. Why run though? Keeping fit, after all, could have been achieved in other ways with an expenditure of much less time and effort. Running, I must admit, was not my first love among sports. It was football, but it needed only a couple of appearances in the school senior team (at right-back and outside-left) to convince me and everyone else that I had better find some other sport at which I might put up a better show. I tried cross-country running and began to achieve success. As someone whose only abilities had been purely academic, it was a revelation. Developing this talent began to give me a very real sense of achievement that provided me with motivation to continue running at school, through university and in the RAF, but would that alone have sustained me in later life when success in competition began to decline? Obviously, I liked the sheer activity of running itself and the enjoyment of simply 'going out for a run' convinced me that running was to be a lifelong pastime of mine until physical disabilities (such as my arthritic knees now!) forced me to call a halt.

There is no use in trying to deceive anyone, however. During that comparatively brief spell of training for top-class competition, no one can run every day in all weathers, as I did, and pretend to enjoy it all the time. At times, indeed, it was sheer drudgery but I stuck at it because I wanted success in the actual race and because I realised that (as I remarked before) it was the training when one did not feel like it that made the difference between the champion and the also-ran. As I have demonstrated, too, in my earlier chapters, it was only rarely that the actual experience of the race itself could be described as pleasurable. The number of times I swore that this present race was going to be my last were many – and yet afterwards, all the pain and discomfort forgotten, only the memories of victory, the triumph of mental and physical powers, remained to tempt me back again.

The real pleasure and joy, therefore, I found in simply running for its own sake – not only physical enjoyment but aesthetic too – the pleasure of feeling the sun on my back as I jogged effortlessly along and my delight in the ever-changing scenery. It was essential that these runs were easy and relaxed. My most vivid memories of them are still a source of very real pleasure for me – in late September the crystal clarity of the sunlight striking low over the golden stubble of the cornfield, later in October the rich flaky chocolate brown of the newly ploughed furrows, or in November and December the silence of the enveloping mist on the hills with the only sound in my solitary world the drumming of my feet on the smooth turf. One favourite run near Stirling took me up two fields steeply ascending towards a gap framed by tall trees on the summit and, every time as I stared up towards the bright sky above that crest, I was seized by a sense of infinity, of being on top of the world, even though I knew full well that it hid only a prosaic cart track winding down through trees on the other side.

The greatest pleasure in these runs was when I was alone and all my senses attuned to my surroundings. Not that I didn't enjoy company, of course! The inter-club runs provided us with a great variety of different scenery on our visits and I enjoyed the camaraderie free from the stress of competition. I made many friends on these runs. I remember especially one wet Saturday afternoon in Stirling when, as I mentioned earlier, I was the only St Modan's runner able to take out the visiting Shettleston Harriers senior pack and I decided to make our run as varied as possible. Unfortunately, the Bannock Burn was in spate as I plunged through the ford, soaking everyone and almost drowning a most irate John Eadie when he was swept away. He and I were later to become great friends to this very day!

Unlike most other track athletes, however, I had to do my training for marathons on the public streets – a factor that had both its advantages and disadvantages. There was, for example, plenty of variety; things were never dull for me and here I was very glad of company to talk to as we ran along. Alone, I was always inclined to increase the pace when I met pedestrians. Nowadays, joggers in our streets are so common as to pass by almost unnoticed. It was a very different story 50 years ago. In the Falkirk district, especially, I was something of a rarity and I cannot even begin to enumerate here the various wisecracks, catcalls and other pointed remarks that were hurled at me by both children and adults as I quickened my pace to pass them. No football referee was ever such a target! Some of the most common taunts were: 'Hairy legs!' 'Awa and buy a bike!' 'You should try a hard day's work!' and, when my run took me near the local mental hospital, 'That's anither o' thae daft yins!' Perhaps the funniest to me, however, were those kind persons who exhorted: 'Go on son! You'll beat Joe McGhee yet!'

Second only to people on the roads, however, dogs provided the biggest distraction – and menace! Besides their continual barking, I was attacked on more than one occasion. It was not the large Alsatian-type dogs that were the greatest nuisances. They soon got used to me on my regular routes and then ignored me. It was the little terriers that were most persistent no matter how often I passed them. I still bear the scars on my right knee after one scurried between my legs at the Boathouse Bridge, Turnhouse. The worst and most embarrassing incident, however, occurred one memorable Sunday morning on the Union Canal bank behind Falkirk when I met a man with two dogs, a large breed and a tiny bitch. The big dog contented himself with a warning growl. The bitch let me pass, apparently ignoring me. Then, without warning, she silently attacked me from behind, almost catapulting me into the canal. I had the seat of my pants ripped right up! My main concern was that, before I could reach home, I had to pass queues of kirk-goers waiting for the bus as I desperately tried to preserve decency and keep my shorts together. But I was hurt most of all, perhaps, by the infirmary nurse's laughter later when she asked where I had been bitten and I replied that I could not sit down!

Nevertheless, as I remarked earlier, my greatest pleasure was to be found in running by myself without the stress of wondering how my companions were feeling. This preference was confirmed one Saturday afternoon when accompanying Willie, a veteran Falkirk Victoria Harrier who had decided to take up road running. We set out on a 16-mile run from St Modan's High School in St Ninians through Stirling to Alloa and then doubled back along the Ochil Hillfoots road through Tillicoultry and Alva. We ran along easily enough, chatting amicably until we had left Alva and were heading towards Menstrie with about six miles of our run still to go. Then, without the least warning, my companion suddenly stopped dead. He looked all right to me, but he said simply, 'I can't go on.' I was then faced with the embarrassing prospect of trying to stop a passing car. (We carried no money for a bus fare!) I had frequently in the past had to reject jocular offers of a lift, but, today, every driver at whom I waved just waved back and drove on. When, finally, I almost ran in front of one car, it stopped. I had warned Willie, 'Don't admit that you're simply too tired to run on. It's a bad advert for the sport.' I then made the excuse to the driver that Willie had pulled a muscle but I refused a lift for myself. I had over half an hour's run still ahead of me through Menstrie, Causewayhead and Stirling before I reached St Ninians. Imagine my surprise, therefore, when I approached the gate of the school and saw Willie just ahead of me, trudging into the main building. He had been dropped in the middle of Stirling at the busiest time of a late Saturday afternoon and had forced himself to try to run briskly uphill towards St Ninians past the football crowds spilling out from Annfield, Stirling Albion's ground, and then, just a little further on, past the visitors emerging from the infirmary. After that, he must have limped very slowly back over the last three-quarters of a mile back to the school. From then on, I resolved, my long road runs would be undertaken alone!

I used to pore over the large-scale maps of Stirlingshire and plan my routes over the quietest lanes and minor roads I could find. I think I must have acquired an unrivalled knowledge of all the little side roads throughout the area. As a student, I had found that the loneliest countryside near my home was uphill to the south of Falkirk and I used to run through the low bushes and scrub of the Blaeberry Mair (i.e. moor), past Prince Charlie's Well on the site of the second Battle of Falkirk (1746), then northwards back through the woods along the line of the Roman Wall at Roughcastle, and even through an exceedingly low and narrow tunnel below the Forth and Clyde canal between Bonnybridge and Camelon. Later, on my long runs, I ventured further south uphill over little tracks across the now deserted moor past the ruins of ancient cottages until I struck the network of little farm roads leading west from Slamannan and then north again to Castlecary. I rarely, if ever, met anyone on these roads and I used to amble along happy and at ease until, reaching the busy roads near home, I was able to speed up to a brisk finish.

Even on my runs between Falkirk and Stirling, I found that I could avoid the busy traffic on the main road by using circuitous minor roads. Running, too, from the school at Stirling gave me even more variety of scenery and solitude on the little roads up past the reservoirs into the Denny Hills, where sometimes I had to splash through fords across the road past the inquisitive cattle and sheep.

Years later, after we moved to Aberdeen, I was to derive similar pleasures jogging by myself, at all seasons, through the woods at Blacktop, north of Bieldside, at times, after a storm, having to climb over tall trees felled by the gale-force winds and blocking the track, or at others glimpsing breathtaking views of the Grampian Mountains, blue in the distance, as the ground fell away at the end of a long ride through the trees.

In Edinburgh, at different periods of my life, I was to live near the Braid Hills but these were so popular with golfers and dog walkers that, to obtain my sense of solitude, I had to run very early in the summer mornings, when the only signs of life were the hosts of scurrying rabbits and sometimes even a fox or two, or on chilly, breath-catching winter days ploughing through the virgin snow.

Beyond the Braids, however, was the challenge of the much higher Pentland Hills and, whether following the paths little wider than sheep tracks along the sides of Allermuir and down towards the distant gleam of Glencorse reservoir or, sometimes further south, climbing straight up over the summits, I adapted my easy steps to suit the slope or avoid the patches of marsh or scree. The magnificent views at every turn of the hill or back down towards the distant city, the silence broken only by the bleating of distant sheep or the lonely, liquid call of the curlew, the freshness of the ever-present breeze on the tops – all these were elements that contributed to my sense of well-being and enjoyment of my run and are pleasures that I now miss so much.

'Yes, but what do you think about when you are on these long runs? How do you cope mentally with such distances?' were questions that I used to be asked frequently. If, immediately on setting off, I were to have thought of the last mile of my run, say from Turnhouse to Falkirk, the prospect would have been extremely daunting. I therefore would deliberately break down the run mentally into separate shorter distances, saying to myself, 'It's only a couple of miles up to Kirkliston,' and then, reaching there, 'It's only another two miles or so to Winchburgh,' and so on to Threemiletown, Linlithgow, Polmont, Laurieston, etc. This ploy was certainly useful but was it enough? Of course, the aesthetic and physical pleasures, which I have been attempting to describe, were also very helpful but were not always present to my conscious mind as I jogged along. I therefore deliberately tried to occupy my mind actively with some topic or other and, indeed, was so successful at times that I would actually 'wake up' nearing the end of a run and could not remember passing through some of the villages and even towns en route. I had developed this technique to handle repetitive or monotonous tasks when working during my university holidays as a groundsman at the recreation club of ICI Grangemouth. One of my tasks, matting, line-brushing and rolling four tennis courts in preparation for the Central Scottish Championships, used to occupy a whole morning. On my first line pulling the roller I would deliberately focus on a topic and then later almost literally wake up on my last line, having beautifully overlapped each line and having negotiated the nets without any memory of having done so. Sometimes, I had been thinking about books (I was studying English literature at that time) but most often I daydreamed about how I was beating Andy Forbes, the then Scottish three miles champion, or John Joe Barrie, the Irish miler.

A few years on, I found that during my long runs the same technique was equally successful. The topic of my thoughts had not to be too serious, however, as trying very hard to concentrate on problems could be self-defeating and I would 'wake up' too frequently, conscious of every little ache and pain. No, most of the time, I suppose, I was a Walter Mitty character, fantasising mostly about how I would defeat the world's best runners, little dreaming that I would one day do so in actuality! As I ran along, my physical movements became unconsciously automatic – so much so that, on a few rare occasions, I actually received an 'out-of-body' experience. After covering about 13 miles of my 15-mile route round Turnhouse airport, for example, I would be running easily along the straight flat stretch between the Maybury crossroads and Barnton and there I would find myself above my body looking down on the smoothly automatic movements of my arms and legs as if they were the actions of someone else. The experience would last only a moment. As soon as I became aware of it, I would be back in my body in conscious control of my actions and feeling all the aches of my efforts again. For those brief seconds, the 'old brain' had taken over to give me the only mystic experiences of my life!

It should be clear by now that, while I may have had a variety of reasons for running long distances, none would have been motive strong enough without the accompaniment of the overriding and enduring one of simple enjoyment. To paraphrase the lines of Charles Hamilton Sorley, a Scottish 20th-century poet:

> *I run because I like it*
> *Through the broad bright land.*

Perhaps, my lifelong passion could not have been better summed up, however, than by the words of another poem by an anonymous writer who sent it pre-war to the late veteran Maryhill Harrier, Jimmy Macnamara, the 1947 captain of the Scottish Marathon Club. He in turn passed it on to Walter Ross, the editor of the *Scots Athlete*, where it was published in 1947.

> *To a Harrier*
> *Some fellow-men seem lucky, yet I*
> *yearn to change with few,*
> *But from my heart this afternoon I*
> *needs must envy you,*
> *Mud-spattered runners, light of foot,*
> *who on this dismal day*
> *With rhythmic stride and heads upheld*
> *go swinging on your way.*
>
> *A dismal day? A foolish word; I*
> *should not years ago,*
> *Despite the drizzle and the chill, have*
> *ever thought it so;*

THE FORGOTTEN WINNER

For then I might have been with you,
    your rich reward to gain,
That glow beneath the freshened skin,
    O runners through the rain.

All weather is a friend to you; rain,
    sunshine, snow or sleet;
The changing course – road, grass or
    plough – you pass on flying feet;
No crowds you need to urge you on; no
    cheers your efforts wake;
Yours is the sportsman's purest joy –
    you run for running's sake.

O games are good – manoeuvres shared
    to make the team's success,
The practised skill, the guiding brain,
    the trained unselfishness;
But there's no game men ever played
    that gives the zest you find
In using limbs and heart and lungs to
    leave long miles behind.

I'll dream that I am with you now to
    win my second wind,
To feel my fitness like a flame; the
    pack's already thinned.
The turf is soft beneath my feet, the
    drizzle's on my face,
And in my spirit there is pride, for I
    can stand the pace.

Postscript

The label, 'The Forgotten Man', was coined belatedly by a tabloid newspaper and used in subsequent headlines in reaction to letters protesting against my Vancouver victory being almost completely ignored by the media (mainly the English-based press), who had concentrated all their attention on Jim Peters's tragic failure. Naturally, these letters of protest came from Scotland, many from my home town, Falkirk, but, oddly enough, one of the most succinct and forceful was written by a London reader of the *Daily Telegraph*, which published it as follows:

WHO WON IT?
To the Editor of The Daily Telegraph

Sir – Never was sentimental irrationality more obvious than in the reactions to the Vancouver Marathon. Sports writers have exhausted their vocabularies of praise for the man who, through unmistakable ill-planning of his effort, failed to win the race. On the other hand, the actual winner, who ran equally well, did not even get his name mentioned. One would imagine it had been a one-man show.

There is no point in running a race if one cannot finish. McGhee did finish, and win. Why was Peters called upon to tear his heart out for a spectacular finale when he knew he had a good 15 minutes in hand?

Sympathy with failure is very well in its way; but it is bad for sport that well-planned, if less brilliant, victory should be passed over almost in silence.

Alan Harrison
Hampstead, NW3

Despite such protests, however, the 'forgotten' sobriquet was to stick. Though the Vancouver Marathon is recalled time and time again – especially when distressing incidents occur over the years in the marathon – the name of the winner is frequently forgotten (as even occurred in a recent interview with Roger Bannister!). Derrick Young, in his book, *The Ten Greatest Races* (1972), indeed, referred to me as 'perhaps the least applauded of all marathon winners' and Norman Giller in *Marathon Kings* (1983) commented: 'McGhee – like the 1908 Olympic champion, John Hayes – became a forgotten man of the marathon.'

In subsequent years, the most significant recognition has come, paradoxically, from England. Chris Brasher invited me to become a member of 'The Awesome Eighteen' (later 'The Notable Nineteen' and now 'The Terrific Twenty-One'), and I have been a frequent guest of the Flora London Marathon at the group's annual dinners.

It has been a different story, however, in official circles here in Scotland. When we first hosted the Commonwealth Games in 1970 in Edinburgh, I was approached about contributing an article on the marathon for the brochure but was told that I would be contacted with further details nearer the time. That was the last I ever heard of it! I did not even receive an invitation to the marathon nor to that in the later Games in Edinburgh in 1986.

POSTSCRIPT

That I was not forgotten by the Scottish public, however, was proved in September 1999, when the *Falkirk Herald* featured me as one of the 'Millennium makers', and then even more so in 2001 when I was voted into fifth-equal spot out of 100 in *Scotland on Sunday*'s poll of Scotland's 'Greatest Sporting Moments'. (The first four were football and rugby teams.) I was therefore rather surprised only a year later to find that I had not been selected for the Scottish Sports Hall of Fame. Even more surprising, however, was the announcement in December 2003 that among 14 new entrants to be admitted was Bobby Thompson, an 80-year-old Glasgow-born ex-New York Giants baseball player who had emigrated to America as a child. No one I have since met had ever heard of him. Nevertheless, Scotland's sporting officials had seen fit to elect someone who had not represented Scotland and had participated in a game not widely played in Scotland. No disrespect to Mr Thompson, but, leaving myself out of the question, I can think of Scottish sportsmen and women – not just athletes – who are widely known and more deserving of the honour. Such is life: there are, however, far more important things to bother about!

This book began with setting the facts right about one race – the celebrated Vancouver Marathon of 1954. It has not been an autobiography, though many details of my experiences in sport have emerged. Other far more important aspects of my life have not really been touched upon – the pleasures (and tribulations!) of my professional career as teacher and lecturer, the privilege of study at three of Scotland's oldest universities and teaching at two of them, the creative stimulus of my writing and, above all, the joys and blessings of family life and friendships.

My mum, in an interview reported in the *Falkirk Herald*, described listening to the radio on Saturday,

7 August 1954 as her 'proudest moment'. Winning the Empire and Commonwealth title is certainly, of course, one of my greatest memories, but my proudest moment of all was 6 July 1960, the day I married Margaret.

P.P.S.
The Myths Continue

BROWSING THE various articles on marathon running on the internet recently (November 2013), I cannot say that I was surprised that many of the myths and absurdities mentioned in the Preface of this book still persist nearly 60 years later. Clearly, subsequent discussions of the 1954 Vancouver race and my part in it simply still build on the highly imaginative and fanciful reports of that time, which I dismissed in the Preface and do not propose to repeat again here. Some new assertions and deductions, however, I must categorically refute.

To begin with, I was certainly not 'preselected' for the Empire and Commonwealth team before the 1954 Scottish Championship. Indeed, at the final meeting afterwards before the team was announced, I was the last to be selected. I was then, of course, the new championship record holder, though one argument was that at least the Scottish colours would be displayed for a considerable time through the streets of Vancouver! Indeed, Dunky Wright, our only previous Empire marathon gold medallist and now a BBC reporter, announced to all the competitors as we lined up for the 1954 Scottish Championship that he would do his best afterwards to argue for the selection of the winner.

In one of these accounts of this Scottish Championship race, it was implied that Jock Duffy, the 1953 champion, was somehow disheartened by my mythical 'preselection' but it did not put him off travelling up from the south of England to compete. However, after my experience over the last miles of the previous year's race when I dramatically cut down on his lead, I had no real fear of Jock. At 10 miles he was 26 seconds behind, by 12 miles Laurence and I had pulled much further ahead of him and he finally dropped out at 17 miles. (See Chapter 2 for a detailed description of this race.)

Another assertion was that the improvement in my performances was due to the RAF supporting me in my training. I did not receive special time off to train. In fact, it was really quite difficult for me at times because I was a section commander and my duties were such that I could only fit in my running at lunchtimes and in the evenings.

Again, my move to Shettleston Harriers was quoted as a reason for my improved road running times. Certainly I was supported by Allan Scally's friendship and advice and by the performances of my team-mates in the shorter relay and cross-country races, but my marathon success was due to my running by myself and my determination to log in more miles, whatever the weather, than any of my fellow competitors.

I could go on, but with the 2014 Commonwealth Games and the 60th anniversary of my win almost upon us, I have no doubt that there will be even more of these fanciful stories of the 1954 Vancouver Games for me to refute if ever I am given the chance!

Bibliography

Books

Amateur Athletic Association Centenary Handbook (London: AAA, 1980)
Giller, Norman, *Marathon Kings* (London: Pelham Books, 1993)
Kipling, Rudyard, *If–* (circa 1885)
Newton, Arthur F. H., *Commonsense Athletics* (London: George Berridge & Co., 1947)
Newton, Arthur F. H., *Races and Training* (London: George Berridge & Co., 1949)
Peters, J.H., *In the Long Run* (London: Cassell & Co., 1955)
Young, Derrick, *The Ten Greatest Races* (London: Gemini Paperbacks, 1972)

Magazines

Anonymous, 'To a Harrier' (Glasgow: *The Scots Athlete*, Oct 1947)
Barber, G.S., 'Athletics in Scotland' (*Athletics Review*, Dec 1958, Vol. 12, No. 8)
Farrell, J.E., 'Running Commentary' (Glasgow: *The Scots Athlete*, Aug 1955 Vol. 10, No. 1&2)
Farrell, J.E., 'Running Commentary' (Glasgow: *The Scots Athlete*, Aug 1956, Vol. 11, No.3&4)

Peters, Jim, 'The Empire Marathon: Jim Peters Own View' (Glasgow: *The Scots Athlete*, Nov 1954, Vol. 9, No. 5&6)

Wilson, Neil, 'The Elite' (London: *Marathon News*, Official Programme Flora London Marathon, April 2003)

'Spotlight – Linford Christie' (*Radio Times*, Aug 1995, Issue 5–11)

Newspapers

Allen, Neil, 'Marathon titans share joy and pain a lifetime later' (*London Evening Standard*, 19 April 1996)

'Athletes told to compete at indoor AAAs or lose money' (*Metro*, 23 Dec 2003)

Barber, Stuart, 'When the going gets tough' (*The Falkirk Herald*, 16 Sept 1999)

Cameron, Donald, 'Marathon winner urgent date' (*Stirling Journal and Advertiser*, 19 August 1954)

'Christie and Jackson maintain rich form' (*The Scotsman*, 20 Aug 1994)

Drysdale, Neil, 'Golden dreams end in cinders' (*Scotland on Sunday*, 28 Aug 1994)

Drysdale, Neil, 'Time to lay down the law and run drugs out of athletics' (*Scotland on Sunday*, 28 Aug 1994)

'Edwards leaves Paris to last minute' (*Metro*, 20 Aug 2003)

'Fifth British Empire and Commonwealth Games Vancouver, 1954' (Report by BECG Council for Scotland, 1954)

Harrison, Alan, 'Who Won It?' (*The Daily Telegraph*, n.d.)

Knight, Tom, 'Going the distance in a new light' (*Scotland on Sunday*, 28 Aug 1994)

'*Scotland on Sunday* Readers Verdict: The Nation's 100 Greatest Sporting Moments' (*Scotland on Sunday*, 7 Oct 2001)

Stevens, John, 'Marathon men break bank for hero Haile' (*Metro*, 1 Nov 2001)
Stevenson, Suzanne, (*Metro*, 5 June 2003)
Walker, Joe, 'A sporting personality' (*Glasgow Observer*, 1955)
'Welcome Home' (*The Scotsman*, 8 Aug 1996)
Wright, Dunky, 'McGhee sets road race record' (*Scottish Sunday Express*, 22 Nov 1959)
Wright, Dunky, 'I know how Joe McGhee feels' (*Scottish Sunday Express*, 8 Aug 1954)

Other Media

Commonwealth Games Coverage, BBC, 27 August 1994
Cram, Steve, (26 Aug 1994, BBC Radio 4) [*Discussion on drugs problem*] [Radio broadcast]